Communities of Meaning

Conversations on Modern Jewish Life Inspired by **Rabbi Larry Hoffman**

Edited by
Lisa J. Grushcow and **Joseph A. Skloot**

BEHRMAN HOUSE
www.behrmanhouse.com

We dedicate this book to our beloved teacher and rabbi, Larry Hoffman, his beloved partner, Gayle Hoover, of blessed memory, and Bonnie and Daniel Tisch, longtime supporters of transformative Jewish endeavors.

—LG and JS

אַשְׁרֵי יוֹשְׁבֵי בֵיתֶךָ עוֹד יְהַלְלוּךָ סֶּלָה:
Happy are those who dwell in Your house;
they praise You forever. Selah.
—Psalms 84:5

A revised version of "Non-Jews and the Jewish Life-Cycle Liturgy" was published in *Journal of Reform Judaism* (Central Conference of American Rabbis, Summer 1990), 1-16. Reprinted by permission of the CCAR.

A revised version of ""From Common Cold to Uncommon Healing" was published in *CCAR Journal*, 41,2 (1994), 1-30. Reprinted by permission of the CCAR.

A version of "Some Jews to Watch in the 1980s" was published in *Moment* (March, 1980). Reprinted by permission of *Moment*.

Published by Behrman House, Inc.
Millburn, New Jersey 07041
www.behrmanhouse.com

Library of Congress Control Number: 2023916124

Design by Tim Holtz
Cover image: iStock.com/hilsajonesen

Printed in the United States of America
9 8 7 6 5 4 3 2

CONTENTS

PREFACE

Lisa J. Grushcow and Joseph A. Skloot

Lisa J. Grushcow is the senior rabbi of Temple Emanu-El-Beth Sholom in Quebec. Joseph A. Skloot is a rabbi and assistant professor at Hebrew Union College-Jewish Institute of Religion.

The essays that follow radiate affection and respect for Rabbi Larry Hoffman, whose teachings have touched generations of rabbis, cantors, educators, scholars, and laypeople. We, as editors, share that deep affection and respect. Among Hoffman's many gifts is that when he speaks to you, it is like you are the only person in the room; he brings the same passionate curiosity to understanding people as he does to interpreting texts.

This book, however, is not intended as a series of tributes (in fact, we had to edit many tributes out, or this volume would be twice as long). The contributors are among those who know Hoffman personally. The goal of *Communities of Meaning* is to show the depth and breadth of Hoffman's ideas and to demonstrate their enduring relevance.

Hoffman is a liturgist who cares about much more than liturgy; a committed Jew who fosters personal and intellectual ties with committed Christians; an academic whose reach extends far beyond the academy. Above all, he challenges all of us—and himself—to constantly rethink our assumptions and stretch our imaginations about what matters in this world.

To pay tribute to Hoffman's reach, the book is organized in three parts. Each part contains essays organized around different themes, and each grouping of essays is prefaced by an excerpt from one of Hoffman's writings, which he selected himself and to which the authors respond.

Part 1, "The Worship Revolution," begins in the area where Hoffman's work is most widely known. From sacred architecture to newly written prayers, from the drama of worship to the challenge of authenticity, from how we use our bodies in prayer to how it impacts our souls, these essays explore all these topics and then some. In teaching us to go "beyond the text" in our understanding of worship, Hoffman opened the doors to consider a wide range of factors that influence how, where, and why we pray. Part 1 shows how his writings provided the scaffolding for considering contemporary questions, like the challenge of communal prayer in a pandemic or the implications of new digital technologies.

Part 2, "Rethinking North American Judaism," shows the wide-ranging impact of Hoffman's thought on Jewish life in North America (although it should be noted that the book's contributors go beyond the United States and Canada to include the United Kingdom, Israel, and France). Grounded in the Reform movement, Hoffman's work on synagogue transformation has influenced all movements. This section includes reflections on North American Jewish life, the future of Jewish denominations, interfaith engagement, and leadership development. Hoffman, as a beloved mentor and teacher and a scholar-in-residence at countless congregations, has unique insight into the landscape of North American Judaism. As a Canadian from a small Jewish community, he has a special eye to the diversity within North America, the unique contributions of the Jewish Diaspora, and the nature of different congregations and their needs. The essays in part 2 ponder what Jewish life looks like today and what lies ahead.

Finally, part 3, "Jewish Behavior and Belief," brings us to the heart of Hoffman's impact. His life's work challenges us to explore what we really believe and how our faith can shape our action. Part 3 tackles those questions. What are the ways in which we understand and misunderstand each other? Where are our areas of faith and of doubt? In many of his writings, from his creative ritual additions to the Passover seder to his teachings about Jewish history, Hoffman advocates for hope; one could even say he embodies a certain Enlightenment hopefulness, which he has held onto as others abandoned it. This is an inspiring stance and also a challenging one. What might it mean to hold onto hope with open eyes? How can we find wholeness in a broken world? These are questions that reach far beyond the particularity of any religion, into our very souls. The contributors in part 3—from Hoffman's more recent students to lifelong thought-partners—rise to the challenge.

What began as a dream, a wish to honor and affirm the teachings of a revered teacher, shared by a small group of students, has become a reality—one more tangible monument to Hoffman's impact and influence. We acknowledge with gratitude our partners in that group—Rabbis Joshua I. Beraha, Jodie Gordon, Evan Schultz, Rachel Shafran Steiner, Daniel G. Zemel—as well as the dedicated efforts of Behrman House to bring it to completion. We are indebted to all the authors featured in these pages for writing thoughtful responses to Hoffman's words and carrying his ideas forward in new ways. Hoffman models the importance of learning as a partnership rather than a solo endeavor, and so it is fitting that the two of us have enjoyed the privilege of working on this project together. Above all, we are grateful to Rabbi Larry Hoffman, for the impact he has had not only on us and on the contributors to his book, but for how he has transformed individuals and communities in meaningful, holy ways.

In his 2011 compendium of Jewish literature from Deuteronomy to David Grossman, *One Hundred Great Jewish Books*,[1] Hoffman wrote with characteristic insight, "Judaism may best be defined as an ongoing conversation." With this book, we dare to add one more volume to that remarkable collection. The give-and-take between Hoffman and his students and colleagues on these pages is a model of that "ongoing conversation" in real time. And just as our teacher encouraged us to fearlessly take our place in that conversation, we ask our readers to do the same: to read and respond to the words and ideas here, to challenge and question, and then to write the next great Jewish book and to expand the conversation. In fact, we believe there would be no greater tribute to Hoffman than that.

The Essence of Blessing

Carole B. Balin

Carole B. Balin is a rabbi, writer, and professor emerita of history at Hebrew Union College.

The room fell silent as the professor, lanky and clean-shaven with a dark head of hair and Coke-bottle glasses, rose to his feet to provide commentary on the morning's sermon and service. Chitchat ceased. Students perched on orange-padded chairs around folding tables festooned with white tablecloths moved, literally, to the edge of their seats—the better to hear the professor. The gathering, like every other communal discussion at Hebrew Union College–Jewish Institute of Religion in New York, took place in the conference-level basement at 1 West Fourth Street in Manhattan. The juicy-colored chairs and matching carpet were meant to freshen up the airless space.

As the professor rose to speak, I couldn't tell whether anyone silently uttered the Talmudic-enjoined blessing upon encountering a sage. But I can vouch for the fact—since I was present at those weekly discussions from 1987 to 2016, first as a rabbinical student and then as a faculty member—that students were in awe of him. They leaned in to scoop up the pearls of wisdom dropped by the man who introduced the Jewish world to the discipline of ritual studies. Dozens of books and hundreds of articles bear his name, Rabbi Lawrence A. Hoffman. Though to his students, to our community, he was always Larry. Simply that.

Hoffman charmed our community with words. He talked *to* people, not at them. His was a conversational tone. His cadence was easy. He peppered his speech with "actually" and "after all." He told relatable anecdotes. He did not use contractions. He repeated the ends of sentences for emphasis. To this day, you can discern in his speech the long vowels of his native Canada, a folksy oratorical marker that turns pretension on its flowery head.

I remember, too, his body language when he spoke at those Thursday gatherings. He would crane his neck in all directions, seeking every eye in the room, an attempt to bring every individual into the conversation. At times, he'd cross his arms as he spoke, slowly rocking back and forth. "The ironic *shuckling* of the Reform Jew," I'd think to myself. More often, he'd plant his left hand on his hip and his right in the back pocket of his khakis—a stance, perhaps, meant to counterbalance the weight of the items packed into the pocket protector of his short-sleeve button-down shirt. He wore nondescript ties and practical shoes. His was the ensemble of a man preoccupied with heavenly, not earthly, matters.

Hoffman thinks big. "I like finding large patterns," he explained, "that no one else sees."[1] For the liturgist, this means applying the social sciences to worship. Thomas Kuhn's "paradigm shift," check.[2] Peter Berger's "social construction of reality," check.[3] Mircea Eliade's "hierophany," check.[4] When, according to the famous midrash, Moses time-traveled to Rabbi Akiva's classroom thousands of years into the future, he was gratified to hear himself being referenced.[5] The rabbis of yore would likewise be pleased were they to have been plunked down on West Fourth on a Thursday to listen to Hoffman opine on the religious and cultural blueprint they designed for Jews to come.

Hoffman took seriously the spiritual formation of his charges. In these pages, students who hung on Hoffman's every word and then blossomed into leaders in the sprawling world of Jewish thought and deed write eloquently about his influence on them.

But what of the influences on Hoffman? How, I wondered, did a self-described naive Canuck who claims he couldn't read unvocalized Hebrew upon his ordination in 1969 become the world's leading expert on Jewish worship? Hoffman and I have known each other for thirty-six years—a good number. When I was a student, he became my mentor, and later, our family rabbi. He blessed and named each of our three children. When I joined the faculty, we spoke often and easily, the give-and-take of supportive colleagues and old friends. But with all that, I had lingering questions about his backstory. So I asked, and he answered.

A "Rabbi-in-the-Making"

Hoffman was his parents' only child and the only kid to attend Shabbat services at the only synagogue in Kitchener, a city in southeastern Ontario that numbered 35,656 in 1942, the year he was born.[6] "I was a shul kid," he said. "I went every week, though once in a while I'd cheat and go to the high school, where they held basketball games on Saturday mornings." He attended by himself because his parents were tied up at his father's podiatry office, where his mother was the receptionist and also did the bookkeeping. But that didn't mean they didn't care about Judaism. They were proudly Jewish, he said, and expected their son to shine as a Jew in their largely Protestant German community. "A lot of people who came to our town after the war wore lederhosen and had names like Horst," he recalled. Their children became his friends when he sat among them in high school classes. Some of their parents were faculty at the local Lutheran college. "They were religious, and I was religious," he said. "We appreciated each other's faith."

As for Hoffman's ancestors, they were from Galicia on his mother's side and from Lithuania on his father's. "They used to joke about my parents being in a mixed marriage," he said. You could also say that he had good *yichus*. His paternal grandfather started a synagogue in St. Catharines, Canada, and attended one of Herzl's Zionist Congresses. His paternal grandmother defied stereotypes of Jewish women of her day and insisted that her three daughters go to college. They all did, thanks to money earned from the millinery shop she established and ran for decades.

The children of Yiddish-speaking immigrants, Hoffman's parents, Ida (Goldstein) and Manuel Hoffman, kept a kosher home on the outskirts of Kitchener. It was a fifteen-minute bus ride to his father's office downtown; from his backyard, Hoffman remembered seeing farms with cows. The house was a modest two-story duplex. They rented out the top and lived below in an L-shaped space that contained a kitchen-dining-living area adjacent to two bedrooms and a bath. Every other week, an issue of

The Reconstructionist Journal, a gift from Hoffman's uncle—Rabbi Morris Kertzer, a disciple of Mordecai Kaplan, who was then working as the first rabbi to be hired by the American Jewish Committee, and who authored the popular primer *What Is a Jew?*—landed in the Hoffman mailbox. Father and son would linger at the kitchen table, discussing its content for hours.

By the time Hoffman started grade school, there were approximately seventy-five families affiliated with the Orthodox synagogue in town, and Manuel decided that the shul was in need of a rabbi—and so was his kid. With the congregation's blessing, he set out for Toronto to make a *shidduch*, a match. Interviews yielded desultory results. "Rabbis came, rabbis went," Hoffman said. But "when I was around ten, they hired a wonderful rabbi. I just loved the man."

Hoffman began to study privately with the newcomer, Rabbi Philip Rosensweig, having attended religious school four days a week to that point. Rosensweig taught by rote. Hoffman said he memorized each word and learned the first three weekly readings of Torah by heart. For his bar mitzvah, he learned how to lead the service and davened Shacharit for the congregation. "It was clear," he added, "I was en route to become something Jewish of significance, and becoming a rabbi was the obvious thing."

What wasn't so obvious was which movement would offer Hoffman the best home. "I tried being Orthodox after my bar mitzvah because my rabbi was Orthodox. My parents were Conservative, though they didn't know it. We were just Jews, with no labels." He laid tefillin daily for two weeks, then gave up and met with a Conservative rabbi in Toronto. Their conversation went something like this:

Larry: *I want to be a rabbi.*
Rabbi: *Do you know* Tanach?
Larry: *No.* (I didn't know the word.)
Rabbi: *Have you studied Gemara?*
Larry: *No.* (I didn't know what it was.)
Rabbi: *Do you know Hebrew?*
Larry: *Not really.*
Rabbi: *Give up the idea. It's too late; you'll never know enough.*

Hoffman's parents sought a second opinion. They found a Reform rabbi, Bernard Baskin, in Hamilton and schlepped their son an hour's drive to meet him. A graduate of the Jewish Institute of Religion,[7] Baskin was the brother of the artist Leonard Baskin and father of the scholar Judith Baskin. They arranged to attend Shabbat services on a Friday. "The service was horrid," according to Hoffman. "We sat in the back. I fell asleep. At the front someone was singing. It wasn't very interesting, you know." After the service, Hoffman approached the rabbi, who towered over six feet. "Ah, er," he began, "I'm thinking of being a rabbi." Rabbi Baskin reached his long arm over him and pulled a pamphlet about Reform Judaism off a shelf. He handed it over, saying, "What a lovely idea. If I can be of help, let me know."

The more Hoffman learned about Reform Judaism, the more it appealed. "The idea of individual conscience made sense to me," he said. "I thought that's exactly what Judaism has to be. You're responsible for your actions. Prophetic Judaism spoke to me. I fell in love with it all, and that's how I got to Hebrew Union College."

Though Hoffman might have known the rabbinate was his calling, he was far less certain about navigating the undergraduate education that would lead him there. He went to the University of Toronto because "that's where all the Jewish kids went." He saw the place for the first time the day after Yom Kippur, on the first day of class. Apparently, someone had driven to Kitchener from Toronto for the holy day and agreed to drop Larry at the U of T dorm the following morning. "I picture myself with a suitcase in each hand," he said, "like an immigrant." Later the same day, at a loss when the registrar asked his desired major, he mumbled, "Sock and Fill," because his ride to Toronto that morning had mentioned that as his own course of study. "Sociology and Philosophy," it turned out, suited him. He did the Canadian equivalent of a BA and then set off to pursue his calling.

The College: New York to Cincinnati and Back Again

On a crisp fall morning in 1964, Larry met his new rabbinical classmate Peter Rubinstein on the sidewalk outside the cold stone seminary with the warm wooden doors at 38 West Sixty-Eighth Street on the Upper West Side. Chiseled into a slightly oxidized metal plate above the entrance were the words "Jewish Institute of Religion" in Gothic script. Nearly a decade-and-a-half since it merged with Hebrew Union College in Cincinnati, JIR became the home base for the two young men, along with five additional classmates. The Cincinnati class numbered thirty-five or so.

As today at HUC-JIR, rabbinical training for Hoffman included a mix of classes and fieldwork. He studied stateside for all five years (the year-in-Israel program would not come into being for another seven years). He remembered studying liturgy with Professor Leon Liebreich, who also taught Aramaic, Psalms, and Midrash. On the first day of class, the professor handed out a syllabus—mimeographed, Hoffman recalled—with typed notes providing the sources and historical background for each prayer. "Our assignment for the year was to look up every single one of them. Look up this, look up that. Don't forget the *Y'rushalmi*, de dah de dah, the *Bavli*. Nobody did it except me." He fell in love with liturgy. "It was the best introduction [to the subject] one could imagine," he added. "I emerged pretty knowledgeable after that. Only because I had done the work."

Hoffman found mentors in two new members of the New York faculty: Professors Martin Cohen and Eugene Borowitz. "Martin's history courses were a balm," he said. "He was a superb teacher, and we read a book a week for him. That's a lot of reading. You'd be amazed how much history you could learn by the time you were done. His political approach to the past was enlightening; it challenged my intellect like nothing I'd ever seen before." Meanwhile, Gene Borowitz dazzled with his lectures on modern Jewish theology. "I loved them," Hoffman said. "They were sharp. You know he knew [the material]. They were deep. I learned more from the two of them than I could possibly have imagined."

While he found his academic studies stimulating, the work in the field was initially fallow. During the first year of rabbinical school, Hoffman's rabbi-uncle hired him to teach eighth grade at the Larchmont synagogue where he was by then the rabbi. "I was a miserable teacher," he confessed. "God help me. The kids were so sophisticated compared to me. I hated the job, and I was out of my element entirely." During the following three years, however, he served Temple Beth Or of the Deaf, which operated from 1961 to 1998. After learning sign language, he became involved in all aspects of the community's life. "I was there every Friday night and Sunday morning. I led services and ran the school. I even attended board meetings." He credited founder Kitty Ebin for providing an education for the hearing-impaired community, as well as valuable lessons in being a rabbi. "She took me under her wing and gave me feedback with love." A brand-new congregation known as the Reform Temple of Putnam Valley in New York reaped the benefit of Hoffman's experience during his final year of rabbinical school.

After ordination in 1969, Hoffman and Rubinstein—best friends since day one—set out for the Midwest to study at HUC-JIR's graduate school. "At the time," Hoffman explained, "they were giving scholarships to recently ordained rabbis who wanted to study further, to train them to teach, perhaps at the College," the affectionate term he used for HUC-JIR. He would trod that path, while Rubinstein would make his way into the congregational rabbinate.

As Hoffman tells it, he completed a doctorate in liturgy largely on his own. He was grateful to Professor Jakob Petuchowski, who wrote extensively on prayer and halachah, for giving him the latitude to do so. As Hoffman put it, "He told me at the beginning, 'These are the courses that I teach. You're welcome to take anything you'd like. But I'm assuming you've already taken it all in rabbinical school.' So they gave me an office—I had an office!—and he just gave me books to read, and I would report to him." Besides taking a few classes with Petuchowski, Hoffman remembered a tutorial on Gaonic responsa with Alexander Guttmann and lots of history with Ellis Rifkin and Michael Meyer. He completed the required coursework, oral exams, and dissertation and was poised to enter the job market within three years of arriving in Cincinnati.

In the past, PhD candidates at HUC-JIR were often "invited" by college administrators to apply for specific jobs. Hoffman was no exception. As he reported, Provost Samuel Sandmel summoned him to his office for "the talk." "Larry," he began, "it's time for you to get a job. There's no sense hanging around here. You've got a family to support. You have an interview this Friday with a friend of mine. Come here at two o'clock. He's going to interview you for Carleton College. You probably never heard of it because you're from Canada. But trust me. It's a very fine institution. It's cold there. You'll love it." The following Monday, Hoffman got a call. Carleton's dean decided to go with an Ivy League graduate.

The truth was Hoffman had long been slated to teach at HUC-JIR. After some discussion of his going to the Los Angeles campus, he remained in Cincinnati to teach for the better part of a year and was then appointed to the New York faculty. He recalled feeling overjoyed when Dean Paul Steinberg gave him free rein to design and teach courses to his liking. In seminars titled "Life Cycle of the Jew" and "Rite and Ritual," he began teaching students how to apply the social sciences to the study of liturgy. He was the first professor of Jewish studies to do so, and he knew what he was doing. Victor Turner, famous for developing the concept of "liminality," once asked Hoffman where he earned his anthropology degree.[8] "I never got it," he answered, whereupon Turner replied, "Keep going. You're very good at it."

Christian clergy, too, cast a spell on Hoffman. "Early on in my career," he told me, "I heard a priest speaking about the Notre Dame Liturgical Center, which was helping the church possibly change its liturgy. They were examining the music and the space, and the choreography too. And I thought, 'Oh my God. That's liturgy? I didn't know that.' This was one of the great eureka moments of my life!" In a similar vein, Hoffman's regular participation in the North American Academy of Liturgy helped shape his scholarship. That he would one day receive the NAAL's Berakah Award—the first Jew to do so—in recognition of his distinguished contribution to the profession affirmed the symbiotic relationship of liturgists, no matter their faith tradition.

Manuel and Ida Hoffman. Rabbi Rosensweig. Faithful Lutheran kids. Uncle Rabbi. The Yom Kippur guest. A pamphlet on Reform Judaism. Liebreich's assignment. Victor Turner. Professor Martin Cohen. Professor Eugene Borowitz. Scholars of Christian liturgy.

Such are the influences that linger over the span of a life.

■ ■ ■

Hoffman gets the final word: The essence of a *b'rachah*, according to one of his articles on the subject, is its intentionality.[9] That is to say that the act of blessing is not a request that God bless an object or action and thereby transform it from the profane to the sacred. Rather, a blessing is an instance for me as a human being to acknowledge the Divine for releasing what is already sacred into the secular space for my use or enjoyment.

ברוך אתה, ה׳ אלוהינו, מלך העולם, שחלק מחכמתו ליראיו.

Blessed are You . . . who shares of [God's] wisdom with those who revere [God].

Rabbinic Artist without Peer

Daniel G. Zemel

Daniel G. Zemel is the senior rabbi of Temple Micah in Washington, DC.

In an age of specialization, the North American rabbi is a generalist. The Bible scholars know more Bible. The Talmud scholars know more Talmud. The historians know more Jewish history. Thus, the new rabbi emerges into the community expected to be a leader, yet as a jack-of-all-trades but a master of none.

Rabbi Larry Hoffman's lifework provides the answer for a true rabbinic calling in the face of this apparent paradox. He expects the American rabbi to be a serious student of Jewish texts and the American synagogue to be a place of serious Jewish learning. And he wants more: his teaching is founded on the core principle that the rabbi's unique focus is to know and understand the community in which they serve. This expertise then becomes the foundation of the rabbi's ability to be a leader. Hoffman's career has centered on creating, teaching, and modeling the tools with which rabbis can understand and lead—tools that can enable rabbinic success in a rapidly changing Jewish world.

And so, as much as Hoffman is a scholar, academician, professor, and liturgist, he identifies himself first and foremost as a rabbi. He is a rabbinic artist without peer. His greatest understanding? The challenge of the modern rabbinate. His community is every student he has ever taught and every rabbi who has read his work. He is a rabbi to rabbis.

■ ■ ■

In the spring of 1984, Hebrew Union College–Jewish Institute of Religion offered rabbinic alumni a three-day program of continuing education, which I attended. It was an opportunity to combine Jewish study and socializing with old friends. At the time, I was finishing my first year as solo rabbi at Temple Micah in Washington, DC, after four years as an assistant rabbi in Minneapolis. On the second day of the seminar, my HUC-JIR classmate Bonnie Steinberg and I searched out and found our favorite teacher, Rabbi Larry Hoffman. I was there to vent and complain.

To that point in my short rabbinic career, I had found no satisfactory place for the serious Jewish learning that I wanted to inform and guide my rabbinate. I was unhappy with HUC-JIR's New York program, even though at the time I could not quite articulate the reasons for my dissatisfaction. I wanted something more—a structure, a curriculum.

I had spent my first year in Washington attending a weekly study group with rabbinic colleagues studying medieval Jewish texts, which had also left me wanting. We would read the text and translate it and, to my mind, pretend that we understood it. The deepest analysis I remember was a comment on the order of "Isn't that beautiful." As a young rabbi, I was a devoted reader of serious Jewish books, but I had no one to discuss them with. They lived alone in my head.

This was how Bonnie and I found ourselves in Hoffman's office, one of us sitting in that familiar overstuffed old chair that we had each sat in so often during our student days. We came to Hoffman as our rabbi, trying to articulate a question that went something like this: How could we be true and full rabbis in our own eyes, not just carry the title?

From this meeting, with Hoffman's leadership, we created an alumni study group—a group of about fifteen of us who would meet three to four times a year and study seriously under Hoffman's guidance.

I dare say that the group was of profound importance to all of us, and I believe more than a few of us could not imagine our rabbinic careers without it. Hoffman's scholarship, learning, intellect, and commitment to the rabbinate stood at the center of it. It provided us with a structured, supportive environment in which to learn and grow. It was serious learning, and it was radically relevant.

As it turns out, Hoffman's academic field of choice, liturgy, made him the ideal teacher for our group of primarily congregational rabbis who were thinking about and leading prayer all of the time. After his own ordination at HUC-JIR in New York, Hoffman had earned his PhD in rabbinic literature. He selected liturgy over Talmud as his area of specialization, but to this day he will tell you that he studies Talmud regularly as a kind of hobby. How else would the consummate rabbi-artist spend his leisure time?

Hoffman created the field of Jewish ritual studies as he moved the study of liturgy far beyond the philology and form criticism that composed his graduate education. [Editors' note: Section 8 of this volume, *"Text and Context"* focuses on this innovation directly.] For Hoffman, liturgy was more than a history of prayer texts. He saw that prayer was the interaction of worshipper, assembled congregation, prayer leader, surrounding environment, and of course the prayer text itself. Moreover, he thought about prayer from the viewpoint of a rabbi struggling to create a vibrant and meaningful worship experience. And worship comprises in turn the setting, actions, ritual objects, music, thoughts, feelings, expectations, and beliefs of all those assembled. Prayer, he taught us, is an act of identity formation. Our study group thus became an adventure in exploring not only rabbinic texts but also anthropology, sociology, psychology, theology, linguistics, and philosophy.

These explorations with Hoffman brought us to a new understanding of our own Judaism and the particular gifts of Reform Judaism. We saw that the European Enlightenment and its quest for universal truths altered the human—and therefore Jewish—landscape forever. Whether using Max Weber's terminology of "disenchantment" or Peter Berger's "sacred canopy," we came to see how the Jews sitting in our sanctuaries were living in a radically different world from their ancestors. The Judaism we fashioned in our communities needed to speak to them.

Hoffman's 1988 lecture "Limits, Truth and Meaning: A Foundation for Dialogue" offers an exciting and innovative structure in which to consider Jewish practice and belief. Hoffman's gift is his ability to interpret religion as a human phenomenon. He is unapologetic about being a non-halachic Jew because he does not accept the premise on which the halachic structure is based—that of law and text divinely and supernaturally revealed to Moses at Sinai. We are left with the challenge to create a Judaism that makes sense to us for our place and our time.

As his book *The Art of Public Prayer* attests, Hoffman's learning led him to conceive of worship as an art form. He then asked: What makes for good art? If we could answer that question, we could then set about crafting meaningful and fulfilling worship that speaks to our era.

This is possible only because of Hoffman's deep and broad intellectual roots and training. When Hoffman considered worship as an art form, we, his students, were challenged to think of our sanctuaries as the setting for a ritual drama that told a Jewish story and inspired the assembled to see themselves as players on the stage of Jewish history. For Hoffman, prayer becomes identity formation, and the challenge is to create an environment and occasion in which worshippers actually feel themselves to be inside a story. We might compare this to the act of watching a play or reading a work of fiction where the viewer or reader becomes wrapped up in the unfolding script or text. Hoffman thus created a new way of thinking about the experience of prayer.

Hoffman's vast learning, mastering a combination of Jewish sources and the giants of secular contemporary thought, enables him to make this breakthrough understanding of how prayer might be conceived. Our study group thus explored his views of Émile Durkheim as having foreseen the challenges modernity would bring to community and the transmission of values. How could we pray our values if we did not fully understand the underpinnings of community? He introduced us to his framework for understanding Ludwig Wittgenstein and the "games" of language as a further way of showing that the way language is used in prayer is a "game" unto itself—that prayers are not mini-theological essays to be understood only rationally. He showed us how to use Claude Lévi Strauss's "binary opposites" as a tool in understanding religious ritual. All of this was in the service of coming to a deeper understanding of our inherited Judaism. Hoffman leaves us with the understanding that our rabbinic role is not simply to continue the legacy of our European forebearers, but also to forge a dynamic, fully American Jewish life.

Many years ago, Hoffman suggested that I read a particular article by Louis Newman, "Woodchoppers and Respirators: The Problem of Interpretation in Contemporary Jewish Ethics." In this essay, Newman refers to the legal scholar Ronald Dworkin. He writes:

> [Dworkin] asks us to imagine a series of authors who write a novel one chapter at a time. Each author (after the first) inherits the work of earlier writers in the series and so is given a kind of limited creative license, for the author's literary imagination must work within boundaries (however fluid) which have been established by previous writers. The need to preserve a sense of coherence within the novel will provide a general framework within which successive novelists will do their work.[1]

I see Dworkin's approach in my work at Temple Micah, and through that notice Hoffman's influence on my work. Just as Hoffman suggested, we are writing the newest chapter of Jewish life. Dworkin reminds me of our need to be rooted. We take our inherited "characters" from previous chapters and plot a new chapter—the one in which we are now living. When we do not recognize this reality, we are not being true to who we were or to who we will be. We are simultaneously in the business of linking to the past while adding our own creativity to this new, future, chapter.

It was Hoffman's framework that gave us at Temple Micah permission to experiment—to write the newest chapter of our collective Jewish lives within the context of honoring and being true to our past and our heritage. And in this way, Hoffman empowered creativity and experimentation in my congregation. It was due to his influence that we at Micah began to think of ourselves as a laboratory of what is possible in American Jewish life. We wanted to step into experimentation proactively, and we wanted the entire Micah community to feel engaged in what we were doing. We became liberated to explore because we felt ourselves to be intellectually rooted.

And Hoffman's impact was felt far and wide—well beyond our Temple Micah community. His devotion to his students and his passion for the potential of American synagogue life moved him to partner with Ron Wolfson to create an independent incubator designed to help synagogues meet the needs of the twenty-first century.

Called Synagogue 2000, it provided an even larger platform through which to experiment, teach, and share a vision of refashioning the American synagogue into spiritual centers—places that were in dialogue with the world outside and where Judaism was, indeed, an ongoing "conversation." The impact of Synagogue 2000 is felt in synagogues across North America today in the music, poetry, movement, even the arrangement of the chairs in the sanctuary.

Then, as though his impact on Temple Micah and on the larger American Jewish community wasn't enough, it turned out Hoffman gave us one more thing—new ways to look at religion itself. As he taught us the need for a new religious language, we learned to read and then think differently. We sought to forge a new language ourselves. Without Hoffman's voice in my ear, I would not have understood from Jurgen Habermas that the merely secular life leaves one "with a sense of something missing"[2] or gleaned from Masha Gessen the felicitous phrase "to reach for a higher note."[3]

In an address to the UJA-Federation of New York, Hoffman observed, "The ... challenge to the [American] synagogue ... is this: Can it speak for the individual drive to plot a life that [matters]? ... We need to balance our emphasis on a community of care with a community of profundity."[4] What, we asked ourselves, is a community of profundity? The search to answer this question has come to animate my work at Temple Micah, as I think it has a world now filled with Hoffman's students and disciples.

Leviticus 21:10 refers to the high priest as *hakohein hagadol mei'echav*, "the priest who is greater than his brethren." This is Rabbi Larry Hoffman, the rabbi who stands above the rest but, in being who he is, lifts us all up and has raised generations of disciples.

My Father's Biggest Fan

Joel M. Hoffman

Joel M. Hoffman is a scholar and author, and the son of Rabbi Larry Hoffman.

Reputation is what matters.

The Greek poet Pindar from the fifth century BCE said so when he wrote that he values a good reputation over great wealth. The Book of Proverbs agrees. So does Rabbi Judah, who in *Pirkei Avot* ranked a good reputation above study, above the priesthood, and even above royalty. And Publilius Syrus wrote in the first century BCE that a good reputation shines even in the dark.

Shakespeare wasn't so sure. While "spotless reputation" is "the purest treasure mortal times afford" according to him, reputation is also a "bubble" that is "oft got without merit and lost without deserving."

The apparent contradiction may stem from a confusion between reputation and image. Though seemingly similar, reputations and images can be opposites. Reputation reflects who we are, while image can work the other way around, with—especially now—image consultants turning people into what they are not. Images are created and crafted, managed and molded, produced and promulgated. Some people do and say what will make them popular rather than becoming popular for what they say and do.

A certain degree of image management is unavoidable. A suit and tie create an image, but so do a sweater and a turtleneck, or a T-shirt; and people generally must wear something. (Wearing nothing would also create an image.) Titles, too, further an image: Doctor or Professor or Rabbi. Or Dad. All of these can be well-meaning approximations of a person, not so detailed as a reputation, but still pointing in the right general direction. Or they can be a smoke screen.

There is, therefore, always a question: To what extent are image and even reputation an honest reflection of a person?

Because I have in some ways followed in my father's footsteps, I've had the opportunity to travel widely in his world. When I do, I frequently meet people who know him and almost always meet people who know of him. And they tell me what they think.

He is considered a brilliant visionary and builder. (Those are even the words I used in toasting him when he retired from teaching at Hebrew Union College–Jewish Institute of Religion in 2018.) His ideas and projects and writings have changed the face of Judaism in North America and beyond. And in so doing, he has shaped the path of the largest and most influential community of Jews the world has seen—a community that he calls his own and that he cares for deeply.

Equally, people know of his spirituality and his compassion. He is known for turning his research into down-to-earth, relatable, and movingly memorable activities and observations. People tell me their lives have been greatly improved by reading what he's written on wellness and illness, for instance, or by hearing him talk about the nature of religion, or by participating in a discussion with him about the role of spirituality in daily life.

"I'm a huge fan of his," people who have never met him tell me. "So am I," I respond with a smile.

This is his image, and it is both flattering and accurate.

Those who know him personally have more detail to add. His students are among the people I most commonly encounter (for he has taught two generations of Jewish leaders). They tell me how influential my father was in helping them find their footing as they forged their professional and even personal paths. They see him as their dear teacher, as well as their treasured mentor, someone who could and would listen with an empathetic ear, and someone who offered advice that combined sagacity and humility. He still makes time to counsel current students and to advise former students who have now become his colleagues and, frequently, his friends.

His commitment to others isn't limited to the classroom or the academy, or to the Jewish people that he so loves, or even to people with whom he agrees. An unrelentless fan of humanity in all its variety, my father devotes energy to the people around him, listening to them, learning from them, guiding them when appropriate, helping them when he can, and always valuing them.

As a result, people of all backgrounds tell me how important my father is in their life—for his support, for his respect, for his humanity and open-mindedness, for his guidance, for his wisdom.

"I'm a huge fan of his," people who have met him tell me. "So am I," I respond with a smile.

This is his reputation, and it is both flattering and accurate.

Beyond the vague image and more specific reputation, obviously, is a human being. I first met him (just as obviously) when I was a young child, when all I could see was the label "father." And as a father, he gave me a fantastically wonderful childhood in what weren't the easiest of circumstances.

The more I got to know him—and I was fortunate that opportunities to spend time with him were bountiful—the more I saw past the label and met the person. In retrospect, I see that his professional life and his personal life share many of the same qualities: devotion; compassion; wisdom, even brilliance; an uncompromising desire to do the right thing, even when it's difficult; optimism; understanding and respect; joy and humor; integrity; awe and fascination with the world; and a steadfast, unrelenting, omnipresent, burning insistence that people are worth investing in.

The people who know him or know of him have hit the nail on the head more than they realize. He is the real thing. The qualities they value in his work reflect his core being and his true self. "If only they knew how right they are," I often think when they sing his praise.

He is my light and guide, my biggest supporter, my study partner, my moral compass, my role model, and my best friend.

And here are his words, the words of Rabbi Dr. Professor Lawrence Ahrin Hoffman—unofficial chief rabbi of the Reform movement, learned PhD who reinvented his field and brought its fruits to the masses, distinguished professor who earned his distinction for the best possible reasons, my beloved father.

I think you'll like what you read, both for the words and for the person they represent. And I should know. I know him as well as anyone alive.

And I'm a huge fan.

Part 1

The Worship Revolution

Section 1

Worship as Drama

Rabbi Larry Hoffman redefined liturgy as a dramatic script through which worshippers enact their identities, presenting them to one another. Since1973, when he first addressed the topic at the biennial convention of the Union of American Hebrew Congregations (UAHC; in 2003, the organization changed its name to the Union for Reform Judaism, URJ), Hoffman has reworked and clarified this concept in a number of public talks. This essay is drawn from these talks. Here, Hoffman's concept of worship as a "script" forms the inspiration for three reflections by Hoffman's longtime collaborators.

However much our worship may be talking to God, it is also an exercise in talking to one another and to ourselves. It is how we voice our hopes and fears, our promises and visions, our shared sense of history, why we matter. Worship is a ritual drama of Jewish identity; the siddur (the prayer book) is its ritual script. Because worship mirrors our identity, the siddur is also a ritual mirror. When a siddur cannot keep up with our changing identity, it is as if the mirror cracks; we no longer recognize ourselves in our prayers, and we declare them irrelevant or worse. Show me a community that worships just as they think they did in the eighteenth century, and I will show you a community that wishes nothing had changed since the eighteenth century. It is the very essence of our worship (and of our siddur that provides the script) to change, because Jewish identity changes.

The ritual drama of worship provides roles: *sh'lichei tzibbur* (worship leaders), a *ba'al korei* (specialist who chants Torah), those called for an *aliyah* (to offer blessings before and after the reading), a *darshan* (person giving the sermon), even the congregation itself, which functions like a Greek chorus. There is also a silent participant, off-stage, whom we call God. The drama has costumes: a tallit, say; it calls for action, too: the *hakafot*, with people kissing the Torah, or shaking the *lulav* and *etrog*, which are sacred props, along with such things as the Torah scroll and a *yad* for reading it.

The siddur is more than a book, then. It just looks like a book because we print it between two covers, but no one looking for Shabbat reading goes on Amazon to find the newest siddur! The siddur is a script for the age-old drama of Jewish identity.

The authors of this drama are the Jewish people through time, including ourselves, the latest generation. The basic plot line, the traditional order of prayer, came from the rabbis in late antiquity, but within that plot line, the actual words of the script have changed through time. In eighth- to ninth-century Eretz Yisrael (the land of Israel), Jews made a festival Kiddush for Rosh Chodesh (the new month)—we no longer do that. In the tenth century, mothers were active participants in the *pidyon haben* (ceremony of the redemption of their first-born sons); Jewish law ruled very clearly that only fathers were commanded to redeem their sons, but tenth-century responsa (rabbinic case law) describe mothers, not fathers, saying *nitchayavnu*, "*We* are obligated," to perform this ritual. Maimonides (1138–1204), living among Muslims, wanted worshipers to take off their shoes before entering the synagogue, and not to recite the Amidah (thrice-daily obligatory prayer) personally, but just listen quietly to the *chazzan* (cantor) chanting it—what would Muslim passers-by think, if they heard the racket of Jews shouting their prayers? There was no Mourner's Kaddish until Christian influence in medieval Ashkenazi Europe. When coffee was brought from Africa to the Middle East in the sixteenth century, scholars like the kabbalists (mystics) of Safed could stay up late, and they invented midnight rituals to keep people piously busy in the dark. We still offer these midnight prayers before Rosh Hashanah and all-night study marathons on Shavuot. They also created Lecha Dodi and

Kabbalat Shabbat—de novo, yesh mei'ayin, out of nothing. *Hanoten Teshuah* ("The Giver of Salvation"), the traditional prayer for the government, goes back through the Ottoman Empire to Spain, but it first appears in a siddur in seventeenth-century Holland, a reflection of the fact that Holland had broken free of Catholic Spain and become Protestant, thereby giving Jews freedom from the Spanish Inquisition.

When printing solidified the siddur's wording, music became the primary way to inject creativity. Eighteenth-century Polish Chasidim used wordless melodies (*niggunim*) to provide ecstatic joy in the midst of poverty; nineteenth-century German Reformers added an organ to reflect the sense that Jewish worship was harmonious with the great cultures of Vienna and Berlin. As the circumstances of Jewish identity evolve, so, too, does our worship, which must accurately mirror who we are, or we stop caring about it.

The siddur is also the diary of the Jewish people, the book in which Jews through the ages have recorded their experience; and not just the diary of the past, but our diary too: the new music and prayers that we add are our own diary entries that the next generation will inherit.

CHAPTER 1

Liturgy as Art
On the Liturgical Artist
Sonja K. Pilz

Sonja K. Pilz is the spiritual leader of Congregation Beth Shalom in Bozeman, Montana.

One of the most central aspects of Rabbi Larry Hoffman's work and presence as a liturgist is the fact that it arouses love. Like few other thinkers in contemporary Reform Judaism, Hoffman and his work are beloved not only by students but also by colleagues within and outside Jewish academia and across all ages of congregants and lay leaders of the Reform movement and beyond. The reason for this love can be found, I believe, in the mechanics of art—and in Hoffman's case, in his liturgical artistry.

In 1984, philosopher Elaine Scarry published a slim, humble book: *On Beauty and Being Just.*[1] The book comes from the field of aesthetics, which she calls a "much-neglected" field of philosophy;[2] it makes two central arguments: first, that beauty inspires replication;[3] and second, that "beauty is sacred."[4] Focusing on the consumer of art, Scarry argues that the experience of beauty inspires the further creation of beauty and calls us to "self-correction and self-adjustment."[5] She also explains that beauty, at its core, is more than just the experience of something pretty. It is the experience of truth, of an expression of balance, goodness, and innocence, in both the purely aesthetic and ethical dimensions.

Scarry's writing echoes that of Union Theological Seminary professor of worship and liturgical consultant Janet R. Walton, Hoffman's long-term partner in thought and liturgical expression. Firmly grounded in liberation theology, in her publication *Art and Worship* Walton advocates for artistic liturgies that are "truthful and . . . original."[6] Liturgical art, according to Walton, needs to raise the praying community's "awareness of the question, a willingness to hear it, and a movement toward change" within their aesthetic, theological, and, perhaps most especially, social world.[7]

Hoffman's work and legacy are not to be found only in his writings. His work entails teaching both in the classrooms of Hebrew Union College–Jewish Institute of Religion and on countless platforms for Reform congregants and those outside the Reform movement, on the bimah and in the classroom. His lectures and publications about liturgy, its history, aesthetic expressions, and emotional meanings, change his listeners' and readers' perception—not only of that historical chapter or prayer, but of Judaism as a whole. Hoffman's words on liturgy are, to echo Walton, *liturgical art*, instilling in his community a perception of Judaism as something meaningful, worthy of protection, rich enough to inspire, deep enough to nourish, beautiful enough to spark enthusiasm. Hoffman's words on liturgy are liturgical art.

Yet if liturgy is art, in the sense that Scarry and Walton describe it, then it must inspire not only enthusiasm but also replication. Where can we see this happening within the Reform movement today?

Art, however, rarely simply occurs. It is most often created, formed, or made by a person—the artist; in our context, the liturgical artist. Our own Reform liturgical culture has been essentially synagogue- and community-based for the last 150 years. Historically, few Reform Jews have established home-based religious practices; even today's liturgical renewals, which often create alternative religious spaces (in bars, concert halls, living rooms, or virtual spaces), seldom lead to increased individual Jewish liturgical practice. While the Reform movement has educated and supported many liturgical musicians, singers, and songwriters, Hoffman's teachings have been singular in their emphasis on liturgical artistry of word and ritual. However, most Reform congregants do not replicate the synagogue liturgies and rituals once they are back home.

So if Reform synagogue practice does not inspire replication in the sense of ritual repetition, what is the nature of the replication it does inspire?

While few Reform Jews pick up a habit of daily davening (prayer) after attending Friday night services, many leave feeling comforted, inspired, proud, guided, amazed, acknowledged, and held by their Judaism. And in those emotions, we can find the "replication," passed on and enhanced in the work of our heart and hands, whether artistic, emotional, intellectual, or political. And it is liturgical artists—artists of words, gesture, symbol, and sound—who either evoke or do not evoke these emotions. Any kind of religious art, but especially the performative and immediately experienced artistic expression of liturgical art (that is, art intended to be shared in a liturgical context), requires an artist who can embody, by means of their own life and character, the values of their religion—a task that Scarry points out requires "courage, honesty, sensitivity and imagination."[8] If liturgical artists do not embody the core values of their religion—even more so if they outright defile them—their liturgical work becomes shallow. It might still be "pretty," but it does not inspire awareness, learning, or a movement toward change.

Services and rituals "work" when the holy takes over, when we voluntarily hand ourselves over to the liturgy—to be changed by it. "Good" liturgical art teaches the act of "handing yourself over," making space for the unpredictable, ungraspable, and ever-surprising presence of holiness in our prayer, and, in doing so, changes both the pray-er and the liturgical artist. For the holy to enter, liturgical artists need to cultivate the courage and sensitivity to hand themselves and their prayers over to the praying community. And, in that act of "handing over," they expose their deepest truths—the core stories of their lives, from the greatest happiness to the deepest pain, the prayer of their hearts in all its raw yearnings and tender gratitude.

What makes a "good" liturgical artist? Someone who is unafraid to hand their art over not only to a community of pray-ers but also to God. Someone who creates art with the intention of being in communication with the Divine. Someone sensitive enough to raise awareness without becoming overbearing. Someone who is dedicating their art to praise, affirmation, lamentation, confession, and gratitude.[9]

So perhaps Hoffman is so beloved because when he speaks and writes about liturgy, he hands himself over. His talks and books are ripe with personal stories and learning; they are spiritual just as much as they are historical, poetic, linguistic, or sociological. Hoffman turns his subject into the center of his life, and his life into an integral part of his intellectual exploring and sharing. He teaches the art of "handing yourself over"—to the community of learners and pray-ers, to God, and also, I believe, to himself—each time he hands himself over to our liturgy.

CHAPTER 2

Worship

A Conversation and a Vision

Janet R. Walton

Janet R. Walton is a musician, author, and professor emerita of worship and the arts at Union Theological Seminary in New York City.

When we pray, Rabbi Larry Hoffman has taught us, we experience moments of truth, of beauty, of fear, of sorrow, of joy, of vision and identity. Members of a congregation provide these moments for each other. At each service, every person contributes a piece of distinctive personal experience. Collectively, we absorb aspects of identity that expand to meet the needs of the present moment. Through singing, speaking, seeing, touching, moving, each person assumes responsibility for expressions of beauty and justice. Together, we experience worship as it provides time and space to feel the breadth and depth of human possibilities as they are expressed in a sacred drama. Worship then is a conversation between and among individuals and communities.

Celebrating the Passover seder in Hoffman's home offers an example of this conversation. When we walk into the room, we see a Haggadah at every place around the table. Every person, young or old, has a part to read or sing, connected in some way to each person's life, to what they do day by day, and to their age. It is immediately clear that this experience will depend on every person's contribution.

The cover of the Haggadah is the next invitation. It might be different every year. With symbols and words, we have come to know that every aspect of the ritual matters—every sound, everything we see and feel, every particular experience. There might also be artistic designs and photos throughout the Haggadah. Some texts are the same and some different year to year. The recitation of the plagues can feel like examples of challenges we know and worry about. Hope is real and urgent, not only about something far away but also something very close to our hearts, now. With symbols and words, we discover that every aspect of the ritual matters—every sound, everything we see and feel, every particular experience.

Toward the end of the seder, there is a moment for each person to share something personal. It may be about loss, a change of job, a graduation, a struggle, a sorrow. As each person speaks, the leader pours a drop of wine into a cup. We see each person's drop mixing with other drops, every person's life connected to each other's. The vision of our world as expressed in our worship enlarges as we hear particular and personal moments. Drops of wine poured into a common cup invite conversation with ourselves, with others, and with God.

Here is a poem Hoffman wrote for his own Passover seder during the COVID-19 pandemic, bringing forward the ideas of hope and connection:

> *The point of Passover is the Spring*
> *The pure sheer gorgeous outrageousness of it all*
> *Hope amid despair,*
> *The destination that our hearts demand and somehow find,*
> *The sun, at last.*
> *For we were slaves in the Land of Egypt*
> *And we went free.*
> *Let Passover be,*
> *Especially this year,*
> *One great booming voice of promise,*
> *The human project rediscovered, come alive, for each of us*
> *In our own way.*
> *Though shut up in our homes,*
> *We meet remotely,*
> *With the miracle of spring to let us know*
> *That every winter ends,*
> *Ours among them.*

Experiences of Passover, and in fact all experiences of worship, depend on forms of artistry. In art critic Jed Perl's words, "The arts offer a plethora of images, sounds, rhythms, themes, atmospheres, characters, narratives and motifs that invite . . . a sea change for our lives. They expand our imaginations, multiplying our possibilities." Art sets responses in motion in "a dynamic between authority and freedom."[1] Through art, we remember what we know and also what we imagine. Art nudges—and sometimes shocks—us into considering something new. In Rabbi Peter Rubinstein's words, artists are "prophets of truth that free us of our biases, that touch our soul, that provide room to consider what we have long considered as true."[2]

When Rubinstein was senior rabbi at Central Synagogue in New York City, he and his team asked Hoffman to help them craft a more meaningful experience of Kol Nidrei for the congregation. The traditional Ashkenazic tune for Kol Nidrei carried powerful memories, but few congregants understood the meanings of the text. How could the experience of Kol Nidrei matter for today? Rubinstein turned to Hoffman. In turn, Hoffman asked the clergy and members of the congregation to think about it with him. He wanted to know about their experiences of the High Holidays, asking, "What do you expect from leading and participating in the High Holidays? What grabs you? What particular memories have stayed with you? How would you describe your experience of Kol Nidrei? How have your experiences of it changed year after year?" He listened, and he wrote.

Since that time, the Kol Nidrei at Central Synagogue is sung and interpreted in three parts at different times throughout the liturgy. [Editors' note: The prayer-poems Hoffman created for that liturgy are included in section 3, "Writing Prayers."] Its meanings are layered: we remember, we bare our souls, we return. The new interpretations are drawn from the lives of the people, past and present and future. These new interpretations create spaces, open more conversations, and expand their visions. They reveal something *about* themselves *to* themselves.

Here is an excerpt:

[We] Jews are well practiced in the art of exile.
How to be at peace wherever we may be,
Secured by goodness, love and learning; gratitude and dignity;
empathy for suffering;
Integrity, and kindness—
The bricks and mortar of authentic Jewish coming-home.
Return, return to these, Kol Nidrei charges,
Before lights go out and the stage is darkened.

Every congregation is responsible for the bricks and mortar of its generation. Each person provides a distinctive contribution to the whole. Regard for one another, telling a person's worth, drawing out and supporting one another's hopes and dreams, is the stuff of our prayer, each story, each life, each yearning. Gathered together, they represent a vision for this moment and the responsibility to pass it on.

The meanings of words and actions count. They evolve. Attending to the multiple layers of words, sounds, rhythms, and actions cracks open insights that urge yet another interpretation. Worship straddles worlds—authority and freedom, tradition and modernity. When we come together, we create moments, make-believe worlds where justice prevails and beauty is cherished. In Elaine Scarry's words, "where the ground rotates beneath us, we find ourselves in a different relation to the world than we were a moment before."

Hoffman could have drawn on his own scholarship to produce an updated interpretation of Kol Nidrei. Instead, he began the process by broadening the human palette. For him, the form and content of this ritual depend on dialogue drawn from within ourselves as well as what we inherit. Feelings, needs, yearnings are the stuff of the moment.

From Hoffman, we learn how to pray—that is, pray with consequences. Our conversations within ourselves, with others, and with God lead us to know how to live. They make demands: to love ourselves and others, to cross uncomfortable boundaries, to embody kindness, to expect risks, to prioritize the human dignity of every person, to imagine and create worlds of peace. Whether at the seder table or during Kol Nidrei, these ritual moments cultivate connections with day-to-day living. We pause; we reclaim what they mean for each of us, now. We see, hear, touch, and make space through artistic lenses. Through them, we trust our hopes. The impossible is possible.

CHAPTER 3

Creativity Is Our Birthright

Liz Lerman

Liz Lerman is a choreographer, writer, educator, and recipient of a MacArthur "Genius Grant" and Guggenheim Fellowship.

The Jewish people have been given extraordinary gifts. These have come to us in the form of scrolls, prayers, laws, songs, stories, rules, and celebrations. We have also been given methods for holding onto these gifts in our minds, our bodies, and our imaginations through rituals made for us by our ancestors, as well as those newly constructed within our families and communities. And yet we struggle with navigating the ongoing task of becoming ourselves. We make decisions about whether to preserve or change what has been bequeathed to us or even divest ourselves of some of those practices that are unfulfilling or harmful. We participate, and we protest.

Years ago, I created a dance called 613 Radical Acts of Prayer. I was interested in expanding our notions as to what constitutes radicalism and what constitutes prayer. The number 613 comes from the magnificent Jewish idea (scientifically inaccurate but nonetheless mystically important) that our body contains 248 organs or bones and 365 sinews, corresponding to the idea that there are 613 commandments, or *mitzvot*, and suggesting that we must use the gorgeous structure that is our body to do abundant good in the world. That dance piece included two acts:

Act I: Protect Us as We Preserve the Original Meaning of Things
Act II: Protect Us as We Change the Original Meaning of Things

Rabbi Larry Hoffman writes about ritual-keeping and ritual-making, and in my work with congregations I am struck by how both keep pushing the boundaries of our understanding not just of prayer and God, but of creativity and its role in preservation and in change. I have personally come to see my own lifelong search for understanding creativity as similar to a seeker's path toward God.

I believe creativity is a birthright. And as we know, birthrights can be stolen.[1] But they can also be won back when we nourish our capacities for being in the present, paying attention, and supporting our own visions and those of the people around us. I have spent much of my life trying to liberate imaginations. The tasks and surprises that emanate from this journey feel quite spiritual.

It is useful to place the words "preservation" and "change" at opposite ends of a horizontal plane and then stretch the horizon in both directions as far as possible. Although one can walk between these poles, I prefer to think of it as hiking, because it is beautiful, demanding, surprising and it requires spiritual, mental, and physical effort. You meet a lot of interesting people and ideas along the way. Depending on the situation you are in, you might find yourself closer to one end than the other. And if you bend that horizontal line into a circle, then often these things occur side by side, almost as if they were next-door neighbors.

Hoffman refers to the siddur as the *script* of Jewish worship. This is a brilliant metaphor to bring into our midst as we try to understand our comfort and discomfort with changes in the liturgy, prayer, and our relationship to our texts. As it evolves, questions rise up: Who is leading us? Who gets to speak, when, and in what language? And what kind of music do we want to hear while we sit together or alone, coming to terms with our ancient and contemporary gifts? Whether prayer itself takes place in a synagogue, or on a walk, or in the library, or at the dinner table, we are in constant relationship to our inheritance and our identities.

I would like to bring to this meditation some language and practices from the world of performance—in my case, dance theater and community engagement.

Technique is a series of practices that train a person to be able to perform, regardless of the context or the pressure in the moment. Technique can imply right and wrong ways of doing things. Technique often presupposes a particular perspective of excellence, and thus it becomes a club—one you can join if you are good enough, and a club of humiliation that is used to hit you if you aren't.

I felt a certain enjoyment in coming into dance by learning and accomplishing bodily technique. However, I have to say that I was sold a lie, in that my classical training was supposed to mean I could do anything. Alas, it turns out that my ballet background precludes my muscles from succeeding at break dancing, hip-hop, and African diasporic forms that rely on weight and freedom in the hips and torso. I can do those things, but it requires changing the very molecules of my muscles. This has led me to see that technique might be related not only to skill but also to power structures and gatekeepers. When we consider what we approve and disapprove of in the ritual practices of our people, we may find ourselves in a battle, with technique used as a sword against those of us who do things differently.

Improvisation is a misunderstood concept that could be one of the most powerful parts of our common experience as Jews. Contrary to most thinking, improvisation is not "do whatever you want"; I think of improvisation as a structure that gives us guidance as to how much freedom of choice we have in any given moment. Yes, we have to agree on the parameters. But a good improvisational score gives freedom and encouragement for individual and communal participation. Many of our worship services are actually quite improvisational. There is extraordinary planning that goes into any service, as well as so many places where you can divert from the expected once it has all begun. For example, improvisation could happen when you say the words or don't, close your eyes or don't, listen or daydream, read ahead or focus on what is happening in front of you. This is even more true with the many varying forms of ritual we give ourselves in our individual lives and within our homes and workplaces—how we greet each other or how we celebrate birthdays, for example. We are consistently improvising rituals, small and daily, so we can move through our lives.

Over many years as artist-in-residence at Temple Micah in Washington, DC, one of my goals became giving our congregation the agency and the inspiration to own the moments of improvisation granted to them both by the leaders of the ceremony and by the gifts handed down through so many generations. Some evenings we spread out all over the synagogue, doing different prayers in different rooms. We always did chaotic circle dances, calling on different groups to take the center of the circle based on birth dates, or number of trips to Israel, or how many years people had been synagogue members. Once, Rabbi Daniel Zemel told an old story of a man seeking a new life. He got lost, and instead of going to a new town, he went back to his own town, thinking it was new. And so we went outside and walked around the block and came back into our beautiful synagogue as if for the first time. When improvisation is working, people can be completely in the present.

Finally, what is a *script*? It is a place, an idea, a score, some words that ask us to go to work by harnessing our imaginations and our creative selves to remake, as needed, the joys, anguish, redemption that is in our story every week. Scripts can constrain us or liberate us. They can represent a singular course with severe limits, and they can be catalysts for abundance. There are scripts within scripts, stories within each word, and gestures to accompany all of it.

How do we keep the script fresh? One way is to embody it through physical manifestations in prayer. We sit, we stand, we beat our chests, we kiss the Torah as it passes by. The words themselves are not the only thing in play.

One way we do it is by asking who is doing the talking, who is doing the praying, and who is doing the moving.

We have been given gifts. We are the people of the book but also people of the body. As Rabbi Zemel likes to say, "If we have been made in God's image, and God is most godlike when God is creating, then we are most godlike when we are creating." We can tap into this creativity every time we participate in Jewish rituals, whether individually or in community: when we gather for our blessings on a Friday night or by the side of a loved one in hospice; when we walk to the river for *tashlich* (the ceremony of casting off our sins during the High Holidays) in the fall; when we march in protest to protect our most important values; and when we sit together in silence on a Saturday morning.

One more story: As a child, I loved going to synagogue with my father on Friday nights, the end of a very long week of labor for him. Usually, he would fall asleep. Secretly, I believed this was the point of a Friday night service: to let my hardworking father get rest in public without shame and within the glory of our received gifts as the Jewish people. Call it a technique for sleep or improvisation as a way to contextualize his rest. Or maybe he was dreaming of a new script as the Hebrew and English song and verse entered and left his body with each breath.

Reimagining Jewish Worship

In 2001, Rabbi Larry Hoffman delivered a keynote address at the annual meeting of the Central Conference of American Rabbis, describing his vision for worship in the new century. Below is a selection from that address. Four responses follow drawing on the different aspects of Hoffman's vision, particularly the ubiquity of digital technologies and ever-expanding notions of inclusivity.

Today's computer is to printing as printing was to orality. But there is always a culture lag between invention and the widespread usage of that invention's full capacity. Movies, for instance, were at first films of people doing what they used to do on stage and just the way they used to do it; only later did Alfred Hitchcock put cameras at angles where the human eye had never gone before. Even today, many people still treat computers like a newer, better typewriter. They miss the point. Despite trace remnants of print mentality, we are leaving the print culture behind. "Book" is a catchall term for handwritten manuscripts, Gutenberg rarities, mass paperbacks, and electronic printouts. But these are not the same things. Technology impacts cultural attitudes: It alters people's relationship to the media they use. We err terribly if we judge tomorrow's prayer "books" with yesterday's prayer mindset.

If the rabbis of antiquity gave us prayer as orality and print gave us prayer as literacy, computers provide prayer that is post-literary. Books separate us into isolated readers; you don't talk in libraries. Computers unite us in chat groups, information sharing, and instant shared gratification. It is only a matter of time until we have no prayer books at all.

You should be asking if I am arguing for what *will* be or for what *ought* to be. The answer is both. The first on empirical grounds and the second on theological principles. Some Jews, it is true, shudder at technology's unavoidable impact. But Jewish tradition overall is not represented by the shudderers.

A theology for the internet will follow. Martin Buber cited a Chasidic master who learned from the telegraph that every word is counted and from the telephone that what it said here is heard there.[1] From the internet, we learn that we all share a single world together. Our liturgy, then, would do well to revive the ethical universalism of classical Reform Judaism, alongside the particularistic revival that followed the Six Day War and practically did away with our emphasis on the prophets. In Wall Street parlance, the ideological market is long overdue for a correction.

We should also think through the reality of God who is present in virtual community—not just the community we physically establish in synagogues each Shabbat, but also the one we intuit beyond the computer screen in e-mails from people whom we have never heard of, across the planet. Our prayers will reflect a participational universe where we increasingly discover, but also determine, the interdependence that connects us economically to human betterment, ecologically to the planet, and theologically to one another.

CHAPTER 4

A Theology of the Internet

Jodie Gordon and Rachel Steiner

Jodie Gordon is a rabbi at Hevreh of Southern Berkshire, a Reform congregation in Great Barrington, Massachusetts. Rachel Steiner is the senior rabbi at Barnert Temple in Franklin Lakes, New Jersey.

Living and leading through a global pandemic has shaped our understanding of sacred community in ways that we are just beginning to articulate. In thinking about a theology of the internet, we do not yet have the necessary perspective to offer a fully formed understanding of how and where God might exist differently in the spaces we currently inhabit.

Looking back on those first months of isolation and lockdown and their proximity to Passover, the metaphor of the *midbar* (desert) emerges as a fitting description. That vast stretch of empty space between here and there is also an apt description for where we, the authors, situate ourselves generationally. Born in 1980, we both clearly remember life before the internet; we wrote our bat mitzvah speeches out by hand. We are not digital natives, though we were early users; our freshman year in college was accompanied by individual .edu email addresses. So too as rabbis, and how we experienced the first two years of the COVID-19 pandemic: not quite new, not quite well-seasoned.

Over the course of these past years, we have been inspired by Rabbi Larry Hoffman's voice—sometimes whispering, sometimes shouting, but always reminding us to write new sentences, whatever technology we may use to do so.

There's a piece of paper that I (Jodie) sometimes think about sending to the American Jewish Archives: a checklist I had written for myself on March 11, 2020, when the pandemic lockdown began. The list outlined all the things I needed to do in order to be ready to close the doors of the synagogue for a period that at the time we thought would be two weeks, maybe three. Among the items was "Plan for 'Virtual Shabbat.'" I put the term "Virtual Shabbat" in quotation marks, and looking back on it, I don't think I had any idea what I meant. My prevailing memory of that first online Shabbat is of an intense feeling of novelty. This was so interesting! What would we do? We couldn't possibly do a whole service (or could we?), and people wouldn't want that anyway (or would they?).

In imagining what it would mean to craft a theology of the internet, it is important to comment on the importance of aesthetics. As rabbis, we were accustomed to the particular aesthetics of Jewish communal life that come tethered to the synagogue. More specifically, we assumed a shared and unified aesthetic (i.e., the sanctuary). While using technology to enhance prayer was not new, its use was amplified and intensified by the COVID pandemic in ways we never could have imagined.

Before the pandemic, we thought we knew what it meant to innovate (Kabbalat Shabbat at Tanglewood instead of in a sanctuary—how novel!). We were sure we had been creative with liturgy, crafting the words and symbolic gestures that shaped moments for people going through all sorts of life-cycle experiences. But not until the pandemic did we notice our one constant underlying assumption: we always assumed that we would do our services together, in the same physical space. We assumed that finding God in community necessitated sitting shoulder to shoulder. We did not imagine that the foundational idea of simply being together, in person, would be taken away. We simply never imagined that we could create a new way of being together. What we learned during over two years of "Zoom rabbi-ing" is that while it is indisputably true that, as Mark Zborowski and Elizabeth Herzog notably titled their book about Jewish life in Europe, *Life is with People*,[1] being "with people" may not always require us to physically share the same room. At first we didn't know to look for God in those digital spaces, and yet, how many times did we find ourselves in front of a screen filled with Zoom boxes and, like Jacob, think, "Surely Adonai is present in this place, and I did not know it!" (Genesis 28:16). God was in those spaces, and we found ourselves utterly surprised.

Space, as it turned out, would be more important than ever—except that now we were dealing with the refraction and overlap of multiple spaces, across individuals' homes, across the country, and even around the world. Hoffman taught us to notice the physical spaces in which we invited our communities to worship. Everything visible should be intentional and necessary, thoughtfully arranged. It might seem counterintuitive for a liturgist to insist that our physical spaces mattered, not just our words, but it made perfect sense. Everything is part of the experience we create: the words, the music, *and* the space. Redefining shared space as we joined together remotely gave another opportunity to put Hoffman's teaching to work.

What space in my (Rachel) family's home would most help my congregation engage in connected, worthwhile, and familiar worship? At first, I chose a corner of my living room; the backdrop was books, a windowsill, and a thoughtfully curated pile of board games. It was a cozy and personal background that seemed to work well for my community. I had successfully created a thoughtful worship space for "us." But this "us" was still being defined in relation to me and my congregation. Like so many of my peers, I had created a space for my community to see that only worked when my family hid silently, in a different room, during Shabbat services.

That led me to rethink not only how to create space, but also how to share it more lovingly and more equitably. How could I create a space that worked for my family *and* for my congregation? I bought a shoji screen and moved to a different room, creating a neutral background without disrupting the delicate ecosystem of pandemic living. I could no longer stage the candles and challah to be seen by all through my camera, but I could lead from a more authentic and connected spiritual place. Hoffman writes that "from the internet, we learn that we all share a single world together." Sharing a world means caring for everyone our actions affect—whether across the country or in the next room.

This attention to making space accessible and conducive to worship (or learning, or meeting, or any other purpose) helps us confront the less poetic truth that not everyone can access this possible shared space. We humbly suggest adapting Hoffman's statement to read, "From the internet, we learn that we all share a single world together. . . and that we must seek out ways to create access points for all." We understand God as that which is bigger than any one person, that which connects and propels all of us and everything. Therefore, a theology of Jewish living whose medium is the internet must insist that this tether, this connector, reach those not already wired in. Who does not have the right technology to join in remotely; who lacks the knowledge to use it? Who does not know if they are welcome; who does not even know that we are here?

These questions are adapted versions of the ones that community leaders have been asking since Sinai. Sharing one world only matters if everyone knows where it is, what it is, that they are included, and why they should care. Perhaps, then, what makes this moment different from others in our long history is that the tether travels not through the conversation of a *beit midrash* (study hall), but through the magic of high-speed and fiber-optic technology. To most of us this tether is invisible, yet it is infinitely capable of creating the kind of connection that the Torah imagined: *all* of us, standing together at Sinai.

Hoffman writes, "We err terribly if we judge tomorrow's prayer 'books' with yesterday's prayer mindset." Likewise, we err terribly if we judge tomorrow's services and rituals and life-cycle moments with yesterday's mindset for what it means to be in community. With each Zoom *bris*, Zoom shiva, Zoom holiday celebration, we changed. The way we learned to connect changed. The way we experienced Jewish life through Zoom took a previously 3D panoramic view and refracted it into many little boxes. Our shared space turned into a kaleidoscopic, up-close view of each person, a view made even more beautiful by each box.

This volume may be its own kaleidoscope, a refraction of the teachings of Rabbi Hoffman. His teachings show us that in writing new sentences, in changing the conversation, we can create transformed and transformational communities. Perhaps the pandemic has forced us to articulate this new language and to tether us to one another in new ways.

CHAPTER 5

The Future of Jewish Prayer

Dan Medwin

Dan Medwin is a rabbi and Co-Director of Growth and Innovation at 6 Points Sci–Tech Camp.

Rabbi Larry Hoffman urges us to reimagine Jewish prayer and theology in light of the transformational impact of technology, both discussing what is essential in Jewish prayer today and dreaming creatively about what it might be tomorrow, so that, in the future, Jewish worship may remain meaningful.

Jews do not easily dismiss legacy technologies for study or worship. We still read from parchment Torah scrolls and pray holding books printed on a printing press, a technology invented six hundred years ago. Rather than replacing these media, we revere them. And yet, we also regularly incorporate newer technologies into our prayer services and spaces, sometimes inspired by our Christian neighbors and the corporate world. Newly constructed or renovated sanctuaries include audiovisual systems with projection screens and monitors. Videoconferencing technology offered a vital connection to Jewish community and Jewish prayer during the COVID-19 pandemic lockdowns, and service leaders regularly use digital tablets. Often, however, this new technology is still being used as books once were: as a vehicle to convey text. We are still wrestling with the most impactful use of new technologies in Jewish worship.

For the last decade, I have developed "Visual T'filah" resources for the Central Conference of American Rabbis. Visual T'filah uses contemporary technology to display liturgy for the community, combined with visual imagery. This work expands on earlier technology that simply projected scanned pages from the prayer book onto a screen, reflecting Hoffman's comment that "many people still treat computers like a newer, better typewriter." Since then, we have learned that once a screen is present in a prayer space, it becomes a blank canvas, a clean slate, or even a window. Visual T'filah today can include scenic landscapes or abstract art as a background to liturgical texts, so that both text and imagery contribute to the prayer experience, such as time-lapse videos of the galaxy during Ma'ariv Aravim (the evening prayer recalling the creation of the universe) or photomontages of the recently deceased before the Mourners' Kaddish. Screens are windows into the past and present, to worlds real and imagined, and thus are a dynamic tool to navigate the complexity of Jewish prayer.

Jewish prayer simultaneously reaches backward, maintaining a connection to all those worshippers who recited those same words before us, and forward, connecting us to those who will recite them in the future. It also encourages the worshipper to reach both inward, with reflection, introspection, and spiritual encounters with the Divine, and outward, connecting to others around the world who are saying the same prayers and, inspired by them to help those in need and the world, as a whole. Perhaps this is why the rabbis of the Talmud required windows in Jewish prayer spaces.[1]

The rabbis fixed and handed down the words of the prayers to aid us in our reaching in these directions, to guide our hearts. Reading the poetry of Ma'ariv Aravim can inspire one to ponder the complexities of the created universe and our vital yet humble role within it. Yet Jewish prayer is not merely about maintaining the traditions of the past, no matter how venerable. Our received texts can be a burden, weighing us down. Contemporary leaders therefore strive to artfully weave these various threads together to create desired outcomes: fostering connections to God and community, to the outside world and the inmost self.

Hoffman invokes the example of film in a different context, that of its evolution over time, but perhaps film can also inspire us in crafting impactful community experiences of prayer. A well-crafted cinematic event can create a communal experience that is enhanced by the shared gasps and laughs. Jewish worship spaces cannot and should not become movie theaters, but thoughtful lessons can be learned from filmmakers about evoking powerful communal emotional responses through shared visual and aural experiences. Imagine if a cohort of filmmakers created short films on the themes of the prayers and the movies were shown in the order of the siddur during or as a prayer experience. The impact could be immeasurable. Connection to God, another important goal of prayer, is also impossible to measure. Metaphors are one tool we use in attempting to grasp the infinite and unknowable God. In earlier times, the metaphor of a "King of Kings" was relatable to those living under an all-powerful royal ruler. Today, technology offers us newer metaphors. Perhaps Hoffman's "theology for the internet" could inspire a new metaphor: "God as Wi-Fi." It is all around us, but we cannot see or feel it. And with the right tools, we can connect to it, to the world's knowledge, and to others around the world.

Another important aspect of Jewish prayer is connecting to community and reaching outward, as emphasized by the mandate that worship should occur in a minyan. Hoffman presciently encourages us to imagine a virtual community that connects us with people "beyond the computer screen . . . across the planet." If in 2001, Hoffman's sense of this revolved around the remote exchange of text through email, today we are just beginning to explore the sense of community we can create when viewing the faces and hearing the voices of others in real time on a screen. In fact, many credit the ability to "convene" and pray over Zoom during COVID-19 lockdowns for enabling shared healing and connection during a challenging time.

If seeing a small two-dimensional representation of an individual can foster a sense of connection and community, we can also look to newer technology to provide an even greater sense of shared presence from a remote location. For example, at music concerts, a small 360-degree camera enables anyone, anywhere in the world, to use a virtual reality headset to experience the event more vividly than video alone would allow. People can gather and interact in a virtual space and still have a sense of presence, of being together. Hybrid services of the future may involve a mixture of 360-degree cameras, VR headsets, and holographic in-person projections.

Given the speed with which Zoom services became the norm during the COVID-19 pandemic, these advances may arrive sooner than we expect. Hoffman writes, "It is only a matter of time until we have no prayer books at all." Perhaps the next revolution in Jewish prayer will come when we no longer need words or even images to evoke prayerful experiences or feelings. Technology now exists to allow us to control computers or prosthetic limbs using only thoughts; simply think "left," and the computer will move the mouse left. Similarly, scientists are working on "telepathy" technology that allows people to share rudimentary thoughts with each other. As this technology develops, we may be able one day to send actual thoughts to one another without having to translate them first into pictures or text.

Sharing emotions or ideas directly may turn out to be one of the most powerful interpersonal-bonding activities imaginable. It will take empathy to an unprecedented level. If singing together in community can provide meaningful spiritual connections with others today, how will sharing prayers directly with others via a brain link affect us? Astonishingly, brains networked together have been shown to act as a single, more powerful brain. Could syncing our thoughts with others' help us to better understand our true connection to one another? And to God?

There is no way to clearly see or understand the boundaries and definitions of future Jewish prayer, but we can glimpse possibilities today that may help leaders shape its growth and direction. With an honest reflection on the historical and present realities of Jewish prayer, we can work toward a future in which Jewish prayer can have the greatest possible meaning and impact on our lives. Hoffman's insights give us guidance for crafting a bright and prayerful future.

CHAPTER 6

Jewish Values Shaped by Sacred Space

Richard S. Vosko

Richard S. Vosko is a Catholic priest and liturgical design consultant for Christian and Jewish congregations throughout North America.

"Where we pray shapes our prayer. How we pray shapes the way we live." I shared this aphorism with the cohorts who participated in Synagogue 2000 (S2K), a trans-denominational project founded in 1994 by Rabbi Larry Hoffman and Dr. Ron Wolfson to transform synagogue life across North America. The ten-year-long project drew in rabbis, cantors, musicians, and administrators from the Reform, Conservative, and Reconstructionist movements.

The S2K curriculum addressed many aspects of synagogue life, including the physical place for public prayer. Hoffman knew of my highly specialized work as a designer and consultant for houses of worship and invited me to join the team of instructors. I presented illustrated lectures in all of the major S2K gatherings, urging the participants to pay close attention to the interior spaces of their synagogues and how they affect the way they worship.

All too often congregations think of a liturgical space in terms of construction, renovation, and maintenance. During S2K meetings, I helped participants explore other significant attributes of a synagogue building, to help congregations reimagine their place of worship. How could the space strengthen their relationships, express their identities, and give credence to their values? More so, how might the spatial setting for the liturgy enable them to engage more intentionally in the act of worship?

Since the early days of S2K, the internet has expanded our sense of space and how we gather for worship. The long-term impact of a hybrid experience of liturgy in any congregation is still unknown but has raised some worry. Although some congregations had an online presence prior to the COVID-19 pandemic, the option became normative as the virus spread and strict protocols limited public gatherings. In a 2022 article in *Tablet*, Wolfson and Steven Windmueller cautioned that "the emergence of online synagogues may prove to be a two-edged sword."[1] On one hand, online prayer services helped strengthen Jewish life during the pandemic, "with many synagogues reporting unexpected increased attendance at services, study sessions, and programming."[2] However, according to the authors, many congregations could suffer because "they do not have considerable funding and staff to produce programming that attracts thousands of people."[3]

Hoffman sees another concern. He has often shared with me that in-person worship for most Jews meant listening and watching a service conducted for them by the clergy. This is a common occurrence in other faith traditions as well. In my religion, Roman Catholicism, the Vatican II Ecumenical Council (1962–65) addressed many topics regarding its role in the modern world. It also clarified what the Catholic liturgy is and who actually celebrates it. In doing so, the bishops recovered the paleo-Christian notion of liturgy as the work of the people. Consequently, the 1963 *Constitution on the Sacred Liturgy* instructed that worship should be performed by the whole assembly with its priests. New liturgical rites were gradually introduced that would involve the congregation in different ministerial functions and with the hope of creating more engaging, interactive settings for worship. Progress has been made in the updating of many church buildings to accommodate new rites that are frequently being revised. Nevertheless, in older church structures, the orientation of the pews remains focused on a distant platform at one end of the space separating the clergy from the congregation. As I write this essay, an alarming development is occurring where some congregational leaders are building new churches that replicate the pre–Vatican II non-egalitarian, hierarchical seating arrangements.

Worship in a communal setting is meant to be a transformative experience not only for individuals but for the community at large. Leaders of worship are entrusted with respecting age-old traditions and emerging customs at the same time they address life's sorrows, joys, and visions for tomorrow. Music, sacred texts, sermons, poetry, art, and architecture are powerful tools of engagement during liturgy. Synchronizing these aspects of worship with technology, room acoustics, color, light, textures, and accessible furnishings and areas is essential in order to create a stimulating environment for worship.

In a primal way, a synagogue building is a symbolic expression of the congregation, its history, and its expectations for the future. Ideally, congregations can make architectural and artistic adjustments to their spaces over time as they grow in their own identity and develop new ritual approaches. For example, early Jewish immigrants to North America copied the architectural styles of synagogues in their homelands just as they strove to retain their languages, songs, recipes, and customs. Gradually, these North American congregations adapted floor plans used by their mainline Protestant Christian neighbors. One illustration is the Akron (Ohio) Plan, which served as a template for the construction of countless synagogues in the United States. It was based on a Methodist Episcopal design that featured congregational seating oriented toward the communion table and pulpit in a chancel or sanctuary. At the back of the congregation was a folding wall, behind which were smaller classrooms. That design was considered to be especially suitable for the High Holidays, when the walls behind the fixed theater-style seats could be opened to accommodate larger crowds.

The adoption of these designs was not universally praised within the Jewish community. Prominent synagogue architect Percival Goodman (1904–89) criticized any synagogue seating plan that mimicked the lecture hall or theater model found in churches, writing, "The only religious actor is the congregation, and this is brought about by the central position of the bimah."[4] Only some North American congregations have adopted this Sephardic plan or a similar prototype, which is a more centralized layout, with the congregants arranged in a choral or antiphonal seating arrangement around the bimah. As more congregational leaders continue to look for alternatives to the sloped floor, fixed seats, and stage model still present in most American synagogues, perhaps this plan offers one possibility.

In his book *The Art of Public Prayer: Not for Clergy Only*, Hoffman devoted a chapter to sacred space, writing that in a Jewish house of worship, "to rely on the box stage effect to frame the action is to kill the sense that people off the stage are part of the action being portrayed. They may watch intently, but it will take a herculean effort for them to internalize the message of the drama as their own, rather than as an unengrossing display of what someone else thinks about reality."[5] Like Goodman, Hoffman questions a fixed setting for worship that includes a long nave with anchored seats facing the immovable bimah. He has argued for a long time that a more flexible seating plan, organized around a central location, would naturally draw the worshippers into a more intimate relationship not only with worship leaders but with one another. It should be noted that a centralized plan also creates a greater sense of ownership of the liturgy. The assembly engages with the liturgical action as participants and not spectators.

Research concerned with spatial dimensions and the impact on human behavior is well-known and has been employed in the design of many places. The way in which we create spaces for living, learning, playing, working, and socializing conditions how we act in those places.[6] More so than ever before, the architectural profession is attentive to many factors when designing a building: renewable energy, sustainability, safety, beauty, purpose, location, accessibility, and inclusivity. However, the design of a house of worship is more than merely a matter of architectural design principles, codes, and local regulations. A synagogue is a living expression of the soul of the community.

Congregations want to emphasize their value systems during worship in order to sustain familiar traditions and emerging identities. Further, a worship space that enables good liturgy and cultivates the importance of the community will sustain that assembly in its spiritual growth. The experience of journeying together, supporting one another along the way, is important especially in times of uncertainty.

A congregation transformed by its own ritual practice is energized to engage with the larger community. Similar to a mountaintop, a desert, or a stream of water, a built sacred space should likewise inspire a congregation to share its values. Conversely, a worship space that excludes worshippers from ritual ownership could unintentionally undermine Jewish teachings about the importance of community, both within and beyond the synagogue's walls.

Another relevant reason for creating more inclusive sanctuaries is the desire to attract younger congregants. A recent report released by the Synagogue Studies Institute shows about a 20 percent increase in young Jewish adults (YJA) aged eighteen to thirty-four. This number is up from the 8 percent in the 2010 study. However, the disappointing finding in the study is that "only 8% of the synagogues surveyed reported 'a lot' of emphasis on YJA engagement."[7] As younger generations rely more and more on social media to establish relationships, this report suggests that congregations have to listen more intently to understand their younger members if they want them to belong.

Generations raised on social media have different needs and expectations in their daily lives and during worship. Dependence on their virtual communities for support and encouragement is as important to young adults as physically associating with a community. Some already feel disenfranchised from religious institutions as they search for a sense of spirituality and purpose, and if the sanctuary and the liturgy do not welcome them or engage them, they will not come back. The worship experience needs to capture their attention, feed their imagination, and challenge them to get involved in their congregations and wider communities.

Spatial settings speak loudly about a congregation's identity and what it believes. An all-embracing congregation invites and includes everyone. It sustains a value system that treats every human being and the planet with care. A worship ambiance designed with everyone in mind has no physical or psychological borders. In Jewish places of worship, no one should feel like they are outsiders. No one should be left behind.

CHAPTER 7

Building Bridges

Prayer as Diversity and Innovation

Yolanda Savage-Narva

Yolanda Savage-Narva is the Assistant Vice President of Racial Equity, Diversity and Inclusion for the Union for Reform Judaism and the Religious Action Center.

In his 2001 keynote speech to the Central Conference of American Rabbis, Rabbi Larry Hoffman explores what it means to reimagine worship in the new century. I believe reimagining worship in the new century will have a direct correlation to the methods people currently use to communicate, as well as to how our sacred texts and prayers are interpreted. Hoffman speaks about changes to technology that will impact worship by creating a metaphoric description of "a theology of the internet." In addition to the "theology of the internet," future technological advances will require us to think about, interpret, and apply text and pray in new and diverse ways, reflecting the diversity of our community. The Talmud specifically teaches us that all people are descended from a single person so no person can then say, "My ancestor is greater than yours."[1] There is also a midrash that teaches us that God created humanity from the four corners of the earth: yellow clay, white sand, black loam, and red soil. Therefore, the earth cannot declare to any part of humanity that it does not belong here, that this soil is not their rightful home.[2] As the Jewish community becomes more diverse, worship will evolve from prayer as orality to prayer as print to prayer as technology and further advances beyond what we can currently imagine.

From the internet, we learn that we all share a single world together. Our liturgy, then, would do well to revive the ethical universalism of classical Reform Judaism. As the diversity of the Jewish community continues to increase, so must our understanding and expansion of what the early Reformers understood universalism to be. As we co-create a new world, there will be a strong need to understand a diversity of perspectives and experiences, while building the bridges that connect us to our greater humanity and shared values. According to the most recent Pew Research Center study of Jewish Americans, 15 percent of Jews between the ages of eighteen and twenty-nine do not identify as white, and 9 percent of Jews identify as part of the LGB population (this percentage does not include individuals who identify as transgender).[3] The same study shows that four in ten Jews are married to a non-Jewish spouse.[4] Moreover, according to a 2014 RespectAbility survey,[5] 233 individuals, out of a sample size of 2,607 Jews (8.6 percent), self-identify as living with a disability. Of that same sample, 594 (22.8 percent) reported having either a family member or a close friend who lives with a disability.[6]

The Pew and RespectAbility surveys provide data that highlight the diversity within the Jewish community, elevating the need to prioritize people who haven't always felt they belonged. Driven by this need, I have facilitated over one hundred workshops, trainings, and conversations that focused on two fundamental questions: (1) What does it mean to create a vibrant Jewish community (i.e., embracing changing demographics), and (2) how do we create a community of belonging (i.e., people from all backgrounds and identities feel a sense of value, meaning, and respect as members of the community)? The brainstorming that takes place during these conversations includes a wide range of topics and often includes questions about integrating new and diverse ideas around how we gather and which rituals we sustain. These are all particularly important topics to consider when addressing how to build vibrant, Jewish communities of belonging. Both of these questions lead to one overarching question: What does it mean to be Jewish in the twenty-first century?

Worship is one possible answer to the question. Many of us find value in the physicality of prayer books, reading from the Torah, and gathering in physical spaces as sacred, me included. Holding the word of God in your hand and gathering to form a minyan is powerful, but it can't be the only way; doing things the way they have always been done is problematic and doesn't allow innovation and creativity. Hoffman states that "we should also think through the reality of God who is present in virtual community—not just the community we physically establish in synagogues each Shabbat, but also the one we intuit beyond the computer screens in emails from people whom we have never heard of, across the planet."

For Jews who feel more of a sense of belonging in synagogues, the current way of worship appears to be very comfortable and normative (e.g., melodies, the faces we see on the bimah). But that experience isn't universally felt. Many Jews of Color report not feeling a sense of belonging in synagogues, particularly when it comes to worship, and younger people in particular feel excluded from the opportunity to share their voices more prominently, challenging traditional ways of worship. Being inclusive is critical in creating a vibrant Jewish community; how we worship has a direct correlation to how—and whether—we engage all parts of our Jewish family. Bringing one's full self to Judaism and worship will undoubtedly bring new ways to pray (written expression as well as art and music), new ways to gather (including virtually), and new spiritual leaders (embracing a diversity of leadership) that allow for full expression of these voices who have previously gone unheard. The way we worship must evolve to create a space that empowers all participants to bring who they are, in all their diversity and authenticity, to Jewish spaces. The critical challenge we face is how quickly and appropriately we can adapt to the change.

Preserving the earth is just as critical to our survival. Solving the climate crisis is a global challenge, but at a time when deforestation and tree clearing are the second biggest cause of global warming, I cannot help but link the creation of new physical books, pamphlets, and other printed materials to the demise of trees that directly impacts climate change. The Torah gives clear instructions that during the *sh'mitah* (sabbatical) year, residents of the Land of Israel must desist from planting, harvesting, or pruning, instead allowing the land to rest and replenish itself. The relationship between inclusivity and sustainability is powerful. Using less paper will help improve the environment as well as provide Jewish communities with incentive to innovate and establish new ways to gather and worship, creating diverse content in diverse ways. Hoffman so eloquently sums it up in his essay with this statement: "Our prayers will reflect a participational universe where we increasingly discover, but also determine, the interdependence that connects us economically to human betterment, ecologically to the planet, and theologically to one another."

As Hoffman writes, the "rabbis of antiquity gave us prayer as orality." I believe the rabbis and spiritual leaders of today will give us prayer as born in diversity and innovation. Both approaches can be valid at once if we can imagine a form of worship that evolves.

The underlying reason for innovation around worship is to set the foundation for creating a true *k'hilah k'doshah*, a holy community—one that puts at the core belonging rather than simply participating. As the world changes around us and we reflect on the work needed to make that change happen, I am reminded of Hoffman's words, "You should be asking if I am arguing for what *will* be or for what *ought* to be. The answer is both. The first on empirical grounds and the second on theological principles."

Writing Prayers

A Kol Nidrei Case Study

Rabbi Larry Hoffman has been both a student of Jewish liturgy and its historical development and an editor of prayer books and a composer of prayers. His work may be read in the Reform movement's many prayer books since the 1970s, including Gates of Repentance *(1978), where his poignant and poetic "Creation to Redemption" service appears.*[1] *In recent years, Hoffman has collaborated with Central Synagogue in New York City to produce liturgies for the Days of Awe. Below is a reflection by Hoffman on that collaboration and his method. The three essays that follow, including one by Central Synagogue's senior rabbi, reflect on Hoffman's contributions and approach.*

People wonder what a "liturgist" is. I usually explain that I study prayers, rather than write them. But over time, I became interested in how to write prayers as well. I've come to think there are three ways in which prayers have meaning:

1. *Official Meaning:* The traditional explanation of liturgical meaning is . . . whatever scholars say it is. When people ask what Kol Nidrei ("All Vows," the opening declaration of the Yom Kippur evening service) is all about, they are usually told its "official" meaning,

what cantors and rabbis learned in their seminary training. But the official meaning may not be what people are after. Telling them that Kol Nidrei is a ninth-century innovation that asks God to annul promises or oaths that we fail to fulfill does not do the prayer justice. Additionally, most of us find that rationale morally troubling as well.

2. *Idiosyncratic Meaning:* We sometimes love (or hate) prayers because of the private, or "idiosyncratic," meanings that they have. Kol Nidrei might remind me of sitting as a little boy beside my grandfather in his old, traditional synagogue.

3. *Public Meaning:* I have been looking, however, for the kind of associations that are not official but also not idiosyncratic. What does Kol Nidrei evoke among whole swaths of people? Surely that is the larger meaning that great prayers have for us. I call these unofficially shared meanings "public."

In 2009, New York's Central Synagogue asked me to compose three prayers about Kol Nidrei. Interviewing people about the meaning Kol Nidrei has for them, I received a variety of responses that fell neatly into three topics: memory, vulnerability, and return. My three prayers are built on these public meanings.

We Remember

Like no other prayer,
Kol Nidrei compels our presence,
And not just us alone,
But the memorized outline, too, of younger years,
The gentle feel of those who tucked us in, who blessed our days, consoled our nights;
And came as we do, on this eve, with memories of their own.

We, tonight, are memories in the making,
Warming seats for others who will remember us
In some Kol Nidrei they shall hear when we are gone.

Present too among us are memories more recent,
Of what we did, or said, or were, or weren't,
Since last year at this time.
Of what we learned or lost;
Of kisses that we gave or got;
The laugh that lovers recognize.

The days of empty wandering,
And wondering
Where God was.
Or knowing with compelling certainty
That God was with us
Even in despair.

Kol Nidrei harbors memory of all this.
Its melody persists, insists,
Commands;
And summons our acknowledgment of time.
What we recall of others past,
And what we vow to leave behind
For others still to come,
Who will remember us.

We Bare Our Souls

Tonight we face our nakedness
Mirrored contemplations of concealed selves
Laid bare of artifice. Backdrop
To a cavernous silence broken only by the quiet chant
Of Kol Nidrei.

This is the time
When consciousness colludes with conscience,
To shatter the delusions with which we cloak our souls.
Tonight God asks us where and what we are.

We creatures fashioned in God's goodness
Are capable of cruelty.
We vessels of God's holiness
Litter others' lives
With profanities of speech and deed and will.

The nakedness of Kol Nidrei's call
Can pierce our mettle,
Unsettling us with echoes of the chaos we have caused,
The brokenness of loved ones, at whose lives we chipped away.

Give us pause to recognize how every year
We choose again
To grow more worn and withered, dry inside,
Or stronger, older, far more resolute,
Awake to what should matter most:
Which shall it be?

Kol Nidrei sounds especially pure
To souls who have lost their way
Or find themselves enmeshed in webs of hopelessness.
God, disentangle us, we pray.
Where we have sinned,
Remove the shame of self,
And make us worthy of Kol Nidrei's melody.

We Return

The accident of mortality
Makes life an interim of expulsion
As quickened dust and ashes,
Bookended by eternities.

We were thrust, at birth, onto a stage
As actors unprepared for roles

We never sought to have.
With every day's performance,
We edge closer to the final bow.

But we Jews are well practiced in the art of exile.
How to be at peace wherever we may be,
Secured by goodness, love and learning; gratitude and dignity; empa-
*   thy for suffering;*
Integrity, and kindness—
The bricks and mortar of authentic Jewish coming-home.
Return, return to these, Kol Nidrei charges,
Before lights go out and stage is darkened.

Tonight the world of things, events, and expectations retreats from
*   consciousness,*
That we may honestly confront what we have been,
where we have gone,
what we are worth,
if we have failed.
We pray that at this time tomorrow night,
When ark doors open for Ne'ilah,
Our final service of these Days of Awe,
We may reclaim the promise we once knew we had;
Tonight, at home with God and with one another, we pause for
*   clarity of purpose,*
En route to that rebirth.

CHAPTER 8

Memory, Vulnerability, and Return

Angela W. Buchdahl

Angela W. Buchdahl is the senior rabbi of Central Synagogue in New York City.

In 2009, when the clergy of Central Synagogue wanted to rethink what many consider the "Holy of Holies," the Kol Nidrei service, we asked Rabbi Larry Hoffman to teach us. He gave us the permission, and the charge, to take risks and think differently about how we might approach this iconic service. He did this in two parts: he helped us add new prayers to our service that created emotional connection and meaning between our ancient liturgy and our modern congregation, and he showed us how to reorder a liturgy that had been fixed for centuries, recognizing that the power of liturgy is not only in the content, but in the ebb and flow, the quiets and the crescendos, of the service as a whole.

Hoffman is a rabbi of rabbis. And a liturgist of liturgists. I am not sure the clergy team of Central Synagogue qualifies as a team of liturgists, but we certainly wrestle with our ritual texts as a matter of practice. For over two decades, we have set aside monthly time to think deeply about liturgical issues under the wise guidance of Professor Janet Walton from Union Theological Seminary. [Editors' note: Walton's essay "Worship: A Conversation and a Vision" is found in chapter 2.]

Though Kol Nidrei is one of our community's most beloved, sacred services, it also presents challenges for the modern worshipper.

If one looks at what Hoffman calls the "official meaning" of the Kol Nidrei, the traditional prayer is not a prayer at all, but a legal formula; it exonerates us from any vows or promises that will be made in the coming year. This seems like a problematic premise with which to begin the Day of Atonement, when we hold ourselves accountable for our actions. For most progressive Jews, the official meaning is thorny, confusing, and its literal translation does not resonate with listeners:

> All vows we are likely to make, all oaths and pledges we are likely to take, between this Yom Kippur and the next Yom Kippur, we publicly renounce. Let them all be relinquished and abandoned, null and void, neither firm nor established. Let our vows, pledges and oaths be considered neither vows nor pledges nor oaths.[1]

In addition, the placement of this prayer in modern times doesn't seem to match its liturgical aim. Why put a peak spiritual moment, let alone the pinnacle, in the earliest minutes of the service, when worshippers are still hustling into seats, greeting each other, not warmed up? When we set about reimagining how Kol Nidrei functions during Central's service, we had to think not only about placement but also about unpacking what makes it powerful.

It was clear that people responded to its melody. Kol Nidrei's simple and memorable opening motif evokes deep Jewish memory—of childhood, relatives long gone, and the endurance of an embattled people. Carried within the music's plaintive plea is the suffering and the resilience of centuries of Jewish history. It is said that the strains of Kol Nidrei helped bring wayward Jews like Franz Rosenzweig and Theodor Herzl back to Judaism. The musical theme, which we recite three times, is in a melody considered to be *mi-Sinai,* as if it emanated from Mount Sinai, meaning at least a thousand years old. We knew that a great deal of the power of this service was in the melody itself.

Our Reform forebears in Germany understood the power of the Kol Nidrei melody, even as they rejected the premise of the annulment of vows. Their solution: retain the melody without the words.

Reform Jews in North America continued to sing Kol Nidrei in Aramaic, but they often did not include a literal translation in their prayer books, or they offered an alternative English text instead. It was not until the publication of *Gates of Repentance* that the Reform movement offered the full English translation of Kol Nidrei to its worshippers. [Editors' note: *Gates of Repentance* was the Central Conference of American Rabbis' 1978 High Holiday prayer book, for which Hoffman served as a member of the editorial committee.] Even then, the text was framed with an opening meditation that could be seen as a defense and was followed by a softened English paraphrasing. So it is not a surprise that many Reform Jews have felt deeply attached to the Kol Nidrei prayer without fully understanding what it says. Instead, they come to Kol Nidrei with their own personal meaning, what Hoffman calls "idiosyncratic meaning"— relating primarily to three themes: memory, vulnerability, and return.

Memory

For many, the sound of the cantor singing Kol Nidrei is the sound of Jewish memory, both ancient and personal. Congregants we spoke with described hearing the melody and feeling connected to something ancient and timeless. They could imagine their ancestors singing it in distant countries. They also shared personal memories of hearing it while sitting in synagogue with their loved ones. It was as if the melody were a mnemonic for Jewish nostalgia and connection across the generations. In response, Hoffman composed a beautiful meditation on this theme, which captured our role not only in remembering but also in being links in the generational chain:

> *We, tonight, are memories in the making,*
> *Warming seats for others who will remember us*
> *In some Kol Nidrei they shall hear when we are gone.*

In the revised liturgy we created for our Yom Kippur eve service, Hoffman's evocative words seamlessly introduced the lighting of a memorial candle and the festival lights that open the Kol Nidrei service.

Vulnerability

For many, the Kol Nidrei prayer represents Yom Kippur's reminder to do *cheshbon hanefesh*, to take an accounting of our souls. To take this holiday seriously, we must each examine our deeds of the past year, lay bare the artifice, confess honestly, and ask forgiveness from those we have hurt. On the surface, this may seem to contradict Kol Nidrei's literal text, which annuls our broken vows and promises without demanding an accounting. But for so many, the sound of the Kol Nidrei prayer inspires the soul-searching that the holiday demands. There is something mysterious about it; its words and melody make us feel more vulnerable and open. Hoffman's prayer "We Bare Our Souls"—written specifically for this service—captures this feeling. Here is an excerpt:

> *The nakedness of Kol Nidrei's call*
> *Can pierce our mettle,*
> *Unsettling us with echoes of the chaos we have caused,*
> *The brokenness of loved ones, at whose lives we chipped away.*
>
> *Give us pause to recognize how every year*
> *We choose again*
> *To grow more worn and withered, dry inside,*
> *Or stronger, older, far more resolute,*
> *Awake to what should matter most:*
> *Which shall it be?*

Return

The final theme that emerged was Kol Nidrei's invitation to return—to others, to our best selves, and to God. A sacred homecoming. This theme matches the original text most closely. *T'shuvah* (returning, turning) is the work of Yom Kippur: acknowledgment, atonement, and improvement. In "We Return," the final of these three prayers, Hoffman reminds us that God desires our return:

> *We pray that at this time tomorrow night,*
> *When ark doors open for Ne'ilah,*
> *Our final service of these Days of Awe,*
> *We may reclaim the promise we once knew we had;*

Tonight, at home with God and with one another,
*   we pause for clarity of purpose,*
En route to that rebirth.

These three beautiful, challenging prayers helped us chart a course to a Kol Nidrei we could both explain and affirm. But we still had that placement problem: reciting a prayer that we think of as the grand finale . . . before the play has really even begun.

In order to capture the full intensity of the melody within the emotional trajectory of the service as a whole, we decided to make the recitation of the traditional Kol Nidrei text the centerpiece of the service, rather than the start. In our reimagined service, we placed Hoffman's first prayer, "We Remember," at the beginning, followed by the lighting of memorial and festival candles and the chanting of the first opening line of Kol Nidrei. Next, we inserted Hoffman's second prayer, "We Bare Our Souls," to precede the Amidah (the central liturgy of the daily and festival prayers), followed by the chanting of a longer section of Kol Nidrei. Finally, after the Amidah and the Yom Kippur liturgy of public confession, we inserted Hoffman's final prayer, "We Return," followed by Kol Nidrei in its entirety with cantor, choir, and organ.

In this way, we created a new Kol Nidrei tradition that escalates, both emotionally and musically, preparing the congregation spiritually for the final, full recitation when it arrives. With these radical changes, encouraged by our cherished teacher, we found our way to a Kol Nidrei that moves our congregation, connects us to history and memory, and holds us accountable for the spiritual work the service demands. Hoffman's invitation to courageous reinterpretation and transformation of our liturgy enabled us to do the true work that this holiday demands of us each and every year and embodied its promise of continued renewal.

CHAPTER 9

A Bridge of One's Own

David E. Stern

David E. Stern is senior rabbi of Temple Emanu-El, Dallas, Texas.

I could not begin to sum up the prismatic effect of Rabbi Larry Hoffman on my understanding of prayer. With his remarkable knowledge in the fields of anthropology, linguistics, and philosophy, Hoffman taught us of language that is signifying, synecdochical, or symbolizing; of speech as performative; of the need to move beyond the text to a sense of the prayer act as dependent on the interaction of a community with space, sound, and the written word. He challenged us to create prayer expressions that will acknowledge, touch, and lift the hearts of the worshipping community.

This chapter describes Central Synagogue's project to reimagine the liturgy around Kol Nidrei, the iconic opening prayer of Yom Kippur. What stands out most for me here is Hoffman's profound commitment to acknowledging the integrity and agency of the worshipper. As Hoffman wrote in his introduction to *Beyond the Text*, "It is not the text, then, but the people who pray it, that should concern us."[1] He argued there that a prayer is only a prayer if worshippers can "appropriate" and "usurp" it as their own.[2]

What happens, then, when we sense that the language of the traditional liturgy is not accessible to appropriation? When, in Hoffman's terminology, the "official meaning" requires a bridge to "public meaning"?

In that situation, most clergy would probably write something or look for something written by someone else that might create that bridge. The simple genius of Hoffman's approach for Central Synagogue lay in asking the people what they think Kol Nidrei meant to them, rather than presuming that he could create that bridge from text to heart. This embodies the rabbinic principle of *puk chazei* ("Go and see what the people are doing") at its best, and it yielded the three powerful themes—memory, vulnerability, and return—from which Hoffman composed the beautiful prayers included here.

But now things get tricky. If we acknowledge that the literal content of the text is only one element in the prayer experience, integrated with music, lighting, the arrangement of worshippers, and the location of prayer leaders, then why should the core poetry of Kol Nidrei require additional poetry beside it or instead of it? Could not the text of Kol Nidrei in an appropriately expressive English translation stand beautifully among these other elements of the prayer experience?

I ask this neither as a traditionalist nor as one seeking to diminish the significance of the worshipper's personal perspective in prayer. Rather, I want to make sure we are granting the worshipper full creative agency. As a designer of worship, how do I know when my well-intentioned bridge, even one based on awareness of worshippers' "idiosyncratic meanings," might obstruct rather than enhance the heart connection I want them to make? Is it not possible that the laying of language upon language might clutter or narrow the very access we are trying to create? Might worship be even more powerful if we were to trust the worshipper to build a bridge of their own?

I root this question in the most transformative idea I learned from Hoffman: the distinction between language as symbol and language as sign. Signs have a direct, concrete, and unambiguous referent: if I want to keep my driver's license, I probably should not lend multiple interpretations to the letters "STOP" on a red octagonal metal sheet attached to a post at an intersection. Symbols, on the other hand, refuse to be tied down to singular definitions and instead serve to create deeply felt emotional resonance. Important for our discussion: the quality of objects as symbols or signs is not inherent. As Hoffman teaches, Shabbat candles are symbols *par excellence* and inspire a range of thoughts and emotions, but as soon as we translate their rich possibilities into a definitive, specific concept ("Light is the symbol of the divine"), we render them mere signs and limit their power.

That is the paradoxical risk of liturgical bridge-building. We seek to translate Kol Nidrei into powerful, evocative ideas like memory, vulnerability, and homecoming precisely so that the words and the moment take symbolic flight beyond the cognitive content of the traditional text, but the liturgist's very act of translation runs the risk of turning the symbol that is "everything-associated-with-Kol-Nidrei" into conceptual signage that may leave us earthbound, ironically depriving the worshipper of agency in creating the very bridge we seek.

What should we do instead? The most powerful element in Central Synagogue's process for me was the act of inquiry. What would it mean to incorporate that process within, rather than prior to, the worship experience itself? I believe this is what many of Hoffman's students have begun to do by including the practice of guided meditation in the worship experience. When we frame a given prayer with a thoughtful invitation to its thematic possibilities and provide quiet time to reflect upon it, we send messages to the worshipper that resonate with the core of Hoffman's teaching: your heart and consciousness are fundamental to the prayer process; we invite you to approach worship as a process of both inquiry and inspiration, rather than prescribed recitation. We invite you to be the wise child of the Passover Haggadah and ask, "What does this mean to me?" In fact, I would argue that an artfully worded frame can serve as a source of public meaning, even as it invites the worshipper into private prayer.

The difference between the approach I am suggesting and the process conducted at Central Synagogue is that inquiry/meditation provides no definitive or common answer, even in poetic form. The inquiry/meditative approach leaves worshippers to their own devices, which is both an advantage and disadvantage. The disadvantage is clear: with the best of intentions, we might not provide enough guidance and, therefore, leave people outside the prayer experience or, worse, leave them alienated and confused by it. But the advantage lies in that same agency: the inquiry/meditative approach invites the worshipper beyond the text but refrains from laying language upon language, and thereby limits the risks of over-determined meaning and turning symbol into sign.

For me, at this point in my own spiritual growth, I would opt for fewer words rather than more, for minimalist external guideposts and greater internal agency for the worshipper. This is partly as an expression of, as the

Buddhists teach, "beginner's mind," of resting in my not-knowing. And it is partly because of the growing significance of silence in both my own and my community's spiritual life, a silence made even more a sanctuary because of the surrounding cacophony of our everyday lives.

That is not to say that the right poetry does not have a vital place in public prayer. I find poetry almost a personal necessity in my own experience as worshipper and prayer leader. The right poetry (or other verbal frame) is analogous to the Jewish mystics' notion of the "garments of Torah," an added layer that paradoxically helps the essence shine through.[3] As Hoffman has written, this is true for a few reasons: poetry slows people down; with its gaps and openings in its layout on the page, it moves people beyond simple truth claims and suggests that "a text might mean more than it seems at first glance to say."[4] To me, the best prayer-poetry serves this synecdochical function: it gives us a tangible part suggestive of a greater intangible whole. Poetry says what it says and more; it springs from the specific without being sunk by it. Poet Marianne Moore wrote that it is the poet's task to present "imaginary gardens with real toads in them";[5] change the word "imaginary" to "imaginative" or "imagined," and I think we have captured the synecdochical function of poetry in prayer.

But prayer-poetry has another important role to play. As contemporary poet and essayist Elisa Gabbert writes, "Poetry leaves something out. . . . Verse, by forcing more white space on the page, is constantly reminding you of what's not there. . . . The missingness of poetry slows readers down, making them search for what can't be found." To compose a line of verse, she reflects, is to write "in the company of the void."[6] This element of prayer-poetry is vital to me. First, it recognizes the presence of the void, the divine mystery in which we compose our lives. Second, the "missingness" in poetry acknowledges the fragmentation and incompleteness that are central to our human experience. And, third, all those gaps both let us breathe and keep us searching. The best prayer-poetry illuminates the openings, in all their "missingness" and possibility, rather than filling them in.

And our best teachers do the same.

CHAPTER 10

How Prayers Mean
Rereading Hoffman

Dalia Marx

Dalia Marx is a professor of liturgy and midrash at Hebrew Union College–Jewish Institute of Religion in Jerusalem.

Rabbi Larry Hoffman explores the rich and multifaceted nature of prayer, explaining that prayers have three types of meaning: official, idiosyncratic, and public.[1] Following Hoffman, I reconsider the multilayered nature of each term and highlight their complexity.

Official Meaning

We often look for an authoritative, official explanation for prayers and rituals. Hoffman mentions rabbis who repeat to their congregants what they heard in seminary. Yet different rabbis have heard and learned different things during their studies. A rabbi ordained at Hebrew Union College–Jewish Institute of Religion will probably address the historical, psychological, or emotional meanings of Kol Nidrei, while a Haredi Sephardic rabbi will probably address very different concerns, such as perhaps its halachic (legal) aspects.

Seeking an "official" explanation of the origin of Kol Nidrei, for example, some rabbinic authorities attribute its composition to the Men of the Great Assembly, which, according to Talmudic literature, constituted the spiritual leadership of the Jewish people during the late Second Temple period. Yet those trained in modern historical criticism may date the traditional text only to the ninth century CE. Different people will draw on different sources for authoritative clarification.

This not only holds true between modes of traditional and scholarly reasoning but also creates variety within each one. For instance, Rav Amram (ninth-century Babylon) and Rabbi Simchah of Vitry (twelfth-century France) offer divergent rabbinic assessments of Kol Nidrei: the first dismisses it as "a foolish custom," while the latter embraces it and provides it with an elaborate ritual setting. Nor do more recent scholars speak in one voice. Further, some maintain that Kol Nidrei developed from the halachic practice of the annulment of vows, others argue that it originated in the realm of late antiquity magical practices, while still others connect it to the early modern Spanish conversos, who, it is sometimes claimed (though this has proved historically incorrect), continued pledging allegiance to their true faith once a year. The liturgist Ismar Elbogen (1874–1943), for example, claimed that Kol Nidrei has very little in common with the content and values of Yom Kippur. Some instead stress its social significance; others, its psychological qualities. And then many late nineteenth- and twentieth-century Reform rabbis tried to replace or even eliminate it altogether (judging from the fact that it is still commonly recited today, they failed).

In light of this diversity of "official" views, can we truly say there is a single "official meaning" of prayer? It seems that all formal explanations are subjective and contextual. The question might be more about power, authority, and status than about objective liturgical meaning: tell me who you read and to whom you listen, and I will tell you the official meaning of your prayer.

Idiosyncratic Meaning

Each of us carries our own memories and experiences that shape the meaning that rituals and prayers will have for us as individuals, our families, and our communities. Yet even the most basic unit, the individual, carries a myriad of meanings from different occasions, circumstances, and life stages. The meaning we personally make of a certain Kol Nidrei service is intuitive and fluid. In my case, it may remind me of the sweetness I felt sitting on my mother's lap in my neighborhood shul or the stress I experienced during my military service, when I had to struggle to hear it behind a *mechitzah* (gender-separating synagogue partition). In other moments, it may remind me of my old boyfriend who was moved, along with me, by the dramatic singing of Kol Nidrei in the film *The Jazz Singer* (1927). All the memories and meanings I connect with the prayer dwell within me simultaneously. Most are subconscious, and their retrieval is often unpredictable and highly dependent on my mood, company, and stage in life.

The individual meaning of a ritual is also shaped not only by personal experiences but also by categories such as gender, ethnicity, and economic status. A woman crowded into a small women's section, struggling to get a glimpse of the service and hear the prayer, will likely have a different experience than that of her twin sister sitting in a spacious sanctuary with her spouse and children nearby and within hearing distance of the cantor. Those who by virtue of their prominence or wealth are seated in the front rows of their temples will probably draw different meanings than those who sit at the back, far from the bimah. Kol Nidrei will probably not mean the same to a regular shul-goer as it does to a person who comes once a year or to a Jew by choice who just completed the conversion process.

Given that the meaning of Kol Nidrei is so idiosyncratic and based on the individual experience, does it truly have any inherent meaning in and of itself, meaning that transcends all individual meanings? Not only that, we also need to ask if all meanings are equal. Could it be that Jewish culture relates to some meanings as "better" or "more authentic" than others? That leads us to the third aspect of Hoffman's understanding of prayer: the "public meaning."

Public Meaning

Again, we need to be specific—to which public do we refer and at what point in history? For example, in the Ashkenazic world, Kol Nidrei has an unmatched importance. It is considered highly sacred and transformative, mostly due to its mesmerizing music, which is arguably the most cherished liturgical melody, encapsulating the Jewish experience in its entirety. In Sephardic-Mizrachi communities, on the other hand, Kol Nidrei does not bear the same gravitas and meaning, partly because it is typically recited in a similar *nusach* (melody) to the rest of the Yom Kippur liturgy. Yet, this is also changing; influenced by its status in the Ashkenazic world, many contemporary Sephardic-Mizrachi cantors are giving Kol Nidrei a more prominent place in their repertoires, including, for some, even using the famous Ashkenazic melody.

All this attests to the multifaceted, multilayered, and rich nature of prayer. Indeed, we should follow Hoffman in asking further what prayers meant to those who wrote them, to those who lead and perform them, and to the congregation that experiences them. We can only imagine and assume what ancient prayers meant to their composers and original leaders and reciters. When dealing with contemporary prayers, we may know more, but still no response can be comprehensive or exhaustive. We may ponder what the prayers mean to the rabbi, to the cantor who insisted on a certain setting, and to the congregation. What do they mean to a congregant who joined the choir only so they could spend time with their spouse, to a person who is visiting a Reform synagogue for the first time after a lifetime in Orthodox ones, to a non-Jewish spouse, to the maintenance staff, or to the police at the entrance of the building? There are so many ways in which our prayers can mean to different people, as well as to the same people in different stages of life or simply on different days.

Hoffman often explains that to be a liturgist is to be more than one thing. Bible scholars, for example, are expected to teach it but are seldom expected to publicly lead its recitation, and of course, no one expects them to rewrite it. A liturgist, on the other hand, studies the prayers but also the pray-ers. A liturgist may often be asked (as Hoffman was asked by Central Synagogue) to compose prayers and to publicly perform them. The three beautiful prayers Hoffman wrote reflect interviews he conducted with worshippers, creating completely new texts based on their profound emotions, modeling for us the richness of what liturgy can (and thus should) be. If he had interviewed Israeli Reform Jews, people in refugee camps in Europe, Beta Israel (Ethiopian) immigrants, or secular kibbutz members, he would probably have composed quite different prayers.

We are fortunate to live in a time when we are called to consider and reconsider all aspects of our lives, and liturgy is no exception. Certainly, reexamining and reimagining worship have taken place throughout Jewish history, but never in such a comprehensive way and never so fast. And it is precisely these intensive processes that demand that we be even more knowledgeable and more generous than ever before. Therefore, we must begin the process by taking a breath, avoiding being too quick to judge, and realizing the complexity and multifaceted nature of the ways in which we address the Divine, our communities, and our souls.

Part 2

Rethinking North American Judaism

Section 4

You Are Here

While he is renowned as a teacher of laypeople in congregations across the country, Rabbi Larry Hoffman's professional home for half a century has been Hebrew Union College–Jewish Institute of Religion. Hoffman's classroom has served as his laboratory for experimentation and exploration. His students have had the special distinction of studying a range of subjects with him, from the history of the Jewish liturgy and ritual studies to practicalities of Jewish leadership. This essay is derived from his lecture on the ideological classification of the various Jewish movements. The responses that follow stake out the ideological positions of Reform, Conservative, Reconstructionist, and trans-denominational Judaism today.

I have always been especially fond of the Cheshire Cat's insight, usually given as "If you don't know where you are going, any road will take you there."[1] It helps also, of course, to know where you are coming from, and at the same time—as someone lacking all sense of direction—I admire those wall maps that announce, "You are here." Before you can get where you are going, you have to know where you come from, but also where you are now.

This last question, "Where are we now?," is actually the most interesting. My first serious attempt to answer it was inspired by the British anthropologist Mary Douglas (1921–2007). Of the many lessons she offered, I valued most a two-dimensional axis of identity that she called "grid" and "group" (figure 1). To be human is to internalize a set of rules (the "grid") and to be governed by compelling personal relationships (the "group").[2]

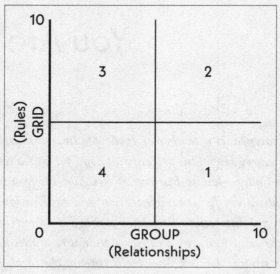

figure 1

Institutions, societies, really any community, can be plotted along the grid and group axis. The most effective societies, those with the maximal social control (and highly controlled individualism), inhabit quadrant two—they score highly on sharing a common set of rules (grid) and on accepting the responsibility entailed by a network of personal relationships (group). The least effective societies, those with minimal social control and maximal unfettered individualism, inhabit the opposite quadrant, quadrant four, where both grid and group scores approach zero.

The point is, modern societies tend toward that fourth quadrant. Douglas called these societies "entrepreneurial" or, sometimes, "the condition of modernity."[3]

With Douglas as my guide, I understood modern Judaism, especially in America, as I never had before. I redrew Douglas's map with our movements overlaid upon it (figure 2).

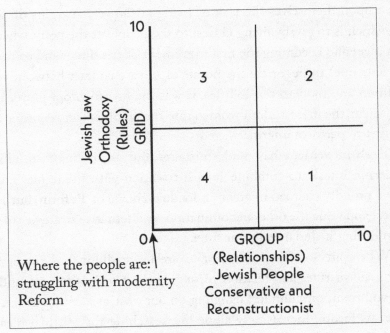

figure 2

If we look at the past century of denominational life, we can see how Modern Orthodoxy specialized in holding fast to halachah—that is, to the grid of rules that has sustained Jewish life since premodern times. Conservative Judaism expressed belief in halachah, redefined as an evolving set of rules that were open to greater latitude in interpretation, but most Conservative Jews do not observe all the rules even in their more lenient Conservative reinterpretation. What these Jews did especially value was Jewish peoplehood. Reconstructionism, founded by Mordecai Kaplan in the 1930s, rejected the exclusive "chosenness" of the Jewish people, but embraced "peoplehood" in the form of belonging to Jewish civilization. Thus, these movements—Modern Orthodoxy, Conservative Judaism, and Reconstructionism—all specialize in one of Mary Douglas's axes: Modern Orthodoxy on the grid axis and the Conservative and Reconstructionist movements on the group axis.

And what about Reform? Reform Judaism was the first to emerge in the cauldron of Western modernity. Ever since then, Reform Jews have taken upon themselves the task of living at the very margins of Jewish life, which is to say, by living closest to the people at the point where the axes meet and becoming the first movement of the three (and sometimes the only one) to negotiate the points of uneasy contact between Jewish tradition and modern sensibilities. It was the first to adopt prayer in the vernacular, the first to admit women into the rabbinate and cantorate, and the first to perform intermarriage.

Each movement has made mistakes, but all of them are allies in modernity's task: to combine Jewish tradition with modernity's allure. I have proudly claimed my own individual choice of Reform, but I fully respect and value the other denominations as alternative strategies to present meaningful Judaism to our time.

Where are we, then? Most of us are in quadrant four, increasingly distrustful of rules and relationships; suspicious of institutions, authorities, and traditions; and left dangling on our own, as a consequence. That leaves us feeling increasingly alone but searching for spiritual meaning and forcing religion to re-present itself, providing a compelling account of where we are, where we have been, and where we should be heading.

CHAPTER 11

A Faith Bounded by Reason

Andrew Rehfeld

Andrew Rehfeld is the tenth President of Hebrew Union College-Jewish Institute of Religion.

Rabbi Larry Hoffman's essay provides a helpful sociological description of Reform Judaism. By framing the movement in terms of institutions and nested relationships—the grid and the group—Hoffman nicely situates Reform Judaism relative to other movements. Yet, sociology is no substitute for philosophy, and here I offer my understanding of the core principles of the movement and its distinctive conceptions of faith, autonomy, and particularism.

Faith

Reform Judaism as a modern approach rejects stories that lack historical or scientific evidence. It rejects these stories because it embraces reason and science as far more reliable paths than faith to understanding our world *as it really is*. No matter how strong our faith in God is, we do not believe the story of Creation in Genesis, the biblical account of Torah being given at Sinai, nor the Talmudic claim that the moon was once the sun, because they conflict with what reason and science can support.

Reform Judaism instead treats faith as *bounded by reason*, operating wherever reason (and science) are silent. Reason and science simply cannot and will not know how the universe arose—not the big bang itself, but whatever came before it (and then before that). Nor can they explain the why of our existence, the meaning of it all. Our faith leads many of us to believe that the universe must have emanated from the Source of All Being, what many call "God," as something outside of the material universe, a first cause of sorts.

Do we *know* that there is a God who has created the universe in this way? No, we cannot *know* that with the same certainty with which we know the earth rotates around the sun. A Reform Jew treats faith as a set of speculative, influential ideas, often felt deeply, concerning the meaning of human life, the nature and existence of the Divine, and the purpose of existence, all revisable based on the findings of science. As reason and science shine light on the knowable world, the scope, implications, and obligations our faith implies will change.[1]

Reform Judaism thus rejects as myths those stories that do not cohere with reason and scientific evidence, no matter how fervently we believe in a Source of All Being. Our faith causes us to believe that our sacred texts were inspired by God, and we study them as sources from which we can derive meaning and purpose for our lives. These texts cultivate a sense of wonder and awe, binding us to our community and to our past. They create a shared narrative, through which we inculcate a strong sense of belonging to a community and sense of obligation to people whom we have not met.[2]

Autonomy

Reform Judaism recognizes that all human beings are morally and religiously autonomous, ultimately responsible for their own decisions. This is based on the moral equality of each individual, the belief in an objective moral universe, and the inherent fallibility of moral judgment.

Reform Judaism recognizes that the moral universe is objective, not determined by our material or social world. Child sacrifice, for example, is wrong whether we live in a society that forbids that practice or not. Reform Jews have faith that the moral structure of our universe is independent of societal norms.

The Reform movement's noble commitment to *tikun olam*, "repairing the world," reflects this objective understanding of moral value. For if values were socially determined, all societal norms would be just by definition, and there could not be societal injustice at all. Our elevation of the prophetic tradition and our recognition that societally entrenched practices like racism are unjust are comprehensible only if ethics and justice have an objective basis that is not determined by society.

Our recognition that morality is objective means our task is to *discover* what is right or wrong, not create it ourselves. And because we are fallible as human beings, we approach moral judgments with humility, rejecting the arrogant certainty that every view we hold is correct. Just as our sages were mistaken about a great number of things, so may we be. (One example of this may be our rapidly changing views of how we treat animals.) We thus adopt care and respect for other points of view, even as we may disagree about the most important moral matters.

Reform Judaism demands that each of us decide matters of right and wrong for ourselves, even as it recognizes that our ability to make good decisions requires education and guidance. We turn to our sacred literature, our teachers, and our clergy for guidance, retaining the responsibility to decide and act for ourselves.

Particularism

If Reform Jews ascribe neither historicity to events nor binding force to the commands recorded in the Torah, that leaves many a Reform Jew asking, "Why be Jewish at all?"

Affiliation with communities is essential to achieving our universal ideals. Joining a community ties us to the lived experience of others with whom we come to identify, cultivating empathy for those whom we do not and may never know. Affiliation with a specific community or nation expands our commitments outward in concentric circles, beyond ourselves and our family, to our friends, our congregation, our people, our nation, and our world. And when those practices themselves include regular reflection on sacred texts within a wisdom tradition, engagement gives us the tools we need to reflect upon and adopt ethical and caring practices.

Cultivating an attachment to a community beyond oneself is necessary because we understand that we all tend to favor ourselves and our own interests unless or until we take action to extend our sphere of empathy toward others. In poetic terms, God may be able to love the whole world at once, but we must first come to love our "neighbor" as ourselves. This insight from our own tradition recognizes that caring for others begins with those nearby—even our own neighbors.

Just as prioritizing the welfare of my own children over the needs of other children does not mean that my children are more important than others', prioritizing members of my own community over those of others does not mean believing they are more important either. Rather, feelings of connectedness through family, community, or peoplehood actually facilitate the realization of our universal objectives.

Reform Judaism thus answers the question "Why be Jewish?" with the answer "Because being Jewish—behaving and belonging as Jews— facilitates the achievement of our ultimate universal aims." We choose to be Jewish because Jewish learning, engagement, and commitment to community resonate with us. In binding ourselves to a community of fellow travelers, we are more effectively able to engage in collective action to pursue justice for all.

But behaving and belonging as Jews is only possible when Judaism itself resonates with us. Jewish liturgy and rituals help us to recognize the beauty and wonder in our world, feel gratitude for Creation and our bounty, and reinforce our commitment to justice. Jewish practices cause us to reflect upon the meaning and purpose of life. Because prayer operates emotionally, we need not affirm the *content* of the words we utter, but, instead, we treat them as expressions of hope connecting us to a long tradition of practice spanning centuries.

The lessons contained within our sacred texts can also resonate and inspire many of us with their wisdom. These include foundational texts of Torah and Talmud and the attempts of Philo, Maimonides, or Buber to incorporate the wisdom of other philosophical traditions into Judaism itself. We also can be moved by the wisdom of modern thinkers like Hannah Arendt, Judith Plaskow, or Rachel Adler, whose Jewish views may stem as much from their encounter with the secular world and our history as from any particular text.

The great challenge of cultivating strong religious and communal attachments lies in fostering a connection with "our own" without losing sight of the universalism toward which that particularism must lead. If we begin to value Jewish study, ritual, and community merely for their own sake, we risk veering into xenophobic, nationalistic, prejudicial excesses that can lead to grave harm in our world.

Because the particularism of Reform Judaism ultimately exists to achieve universal values, Reform Judaism is able to honor without prejudice other intrinsically valuable religious traditions that similarly offer practices that ground their adherents in a rich community pursuing our shared universal aims.

Returning to Hoffman's final challenge, "providing a compelling account of where we are, where we have been, and where we should be heading," the authenticity of Reform Judaism is realized only when we accept these obligations to Jewish life as real and potent. That means not just celebrating our freedom to choose, but exercising that choice by voluntarily accepting obligations to study, engage in ritual, and belong.

CHAPTER 12

To Be a Jewish Community, Worthy of That Name

Arnold M. Eisen

Arnold M. Eisen is chancellor emeritus and professor of Jewish thought at the Jewish Theological Seminary.

Few thinkers of my acquaintance possess greater ability than Rabbi Larry Hoffman to make surprising connections that bring new light to oft-trodden territory. In his essay, Hoffman draws on the work of both the novelist Lewis Carroll and the anthropologist Mary Douglas to provide new insights into the denominational history of American Judaism. Hoffman's conclusion is striking both in its optimism and in its concluding warning about the current state of American Judaism and the American Jewish community. What we need, and sorely lack, Hoffman writes, is "a compelling account of where we are, where we have been, and where we should be heading."

I have always found Solomon Schechter (1847–1915) to be a partic-ularly helpful guide to that threefold task. Schechter was the chief trans-mitter to America of "positive-historical Judaism," the European forebear of the Conservative movement, most importantly through his work as founding president of the reorganized Jewish Theological Seminary (JTS). That role, in turn, led Schechter to form (somewhat reluctantly) the rabbinic and congregational arms of Conservative Judaism, with the dual aim of serving JTS alumni and strengthening Jewish life in America as a whole. Schechter was no fan of sectarianism; he was committed to Jewish unity, a concept he famously referred to as "Catholic Israel," a living entity responsible for authoritatively "teaching and developing the word of God" embodied in the "Universal Synagogue." That "center of authority" for authentic Judaism, he emphasized, "is not represented by any section of the nation, or any corporate priesthood, or Rabbihood [*sic*], but by the collective conscience of Catholic Israel," drawing upon a long succession of "Prophets, Scribes ... and Teachers." Schechter lovingly named the links in the chain of tradition at length and ennobled every one of them by spelling it with a capital letter.[1]

Schechter's appeal to Catholic Israel is at once razor-sharp and at the same time studiously vague. He praises the attitude of "enlightened Scepticism combined with a staunch conservatism" that he finds in the positive historical school. To reconcile that difficult combination, Schechter explained that the key underlying claim is this: "It is not the mere revealed Bible [!!] that is of first importance to the Jew, but the Bible as it repeats itself in history, in other words, as it is interpreted by Tradition." No less important, Schechter attributes this "Secondary Meaning"—the interpretive tradition—not to internal developments in Jewish law or thought, but to "changing historical influences."[2] Judaism has changed significantly over time, yet somehow remained identifiably itself. That balancing act, Schechter implies, is not easily accomplished, and it may be harder in modern times than ever before. But it *can be* done, *has been* done, and *will be* done far into the future—so long as "Catholic Israel" accepts responsibility for doing it.

Schechter would say that the principal task facing Jews today—as in any day since the rise of rabbinic Judaism—is authentic transmission of *tradition,* the key term in his view of Judaism. Having moved the center of gravity from the Bible to the sages, Schechter called on Jews of his day to do what they and their predecessors had done over the centuries. That mission involved both "skepticism" and "conservatism"; that is, both innovation born of changing historical circumstances and fidelity to tradition in thought and practice.

Who was included in Catholic Israel, as Schechter saw it, and who was not? The answer is not entirely clear, in keeping with both Schechter's intentions and the nature of the task at hand. Jews who utterly denied the facts of history—we would call these Jews "ultra-Orthodox" today—would seem to be outside the circle of authenticity on that score but inside by virtue of their learning and observance. "Classical Reform" Jews of Schechter's day were also outside because of their willingness to dispense with Jewish law in the name of modernity but inside because they knew Judaism had always changed and were open to changing it further.

It is telling that Schechter titled his 1913 address at the Reform movement's Hebrew Union College in Cincinnati "His Majesty's Opposition," a term British parliamentarians gave to their opponents. As Schechter explained, despite their differences, the two sides "form one large community, working for the welfare of the country and the prosperity of the nation."[3] I believe that Schechter wanted to urge his audience of Reform Jews to become learned and observant enough to be included in Catholic Israel.

The key takeaway from Schechter, I think, should not be awarding "points" to various denominations for authenticity or viability. Rather, we must identify what all Jews need to do if they are committed to the survival and thriving of the Jewish people and the Jewish tradition—the twin components of "Catholic Israel" and the "Universal Synagogue." In a 1903 address at JTS, Schechter asked his audience what factors united the students of the medieval scholars Rashi and Maimonides. His answer: shared fasts and feasts; reverence for the same sacred symbols, albeit differently interpreted; prayer in the same language, Hebrew; study of the same Torah; admiration for Israel's past, albeit with differing views of key events such as Revelation; and longing for Israel's future redemption—"they studied the Torah and lived in accordance with its laws, and made the hopes of the Jewish nation their own."[4]

Schechter's list still serves us well, and as Hoffman's denominational chart makes clear, no one-dimensional spectrum of authenticity—commonly drawn with Reform and Reconstructionism at one end, Modern and Traditionalist Orthodoxy at the other, and the various sorts of Conservative Jews like me in the center—will suffice. Multidimensional analysis is required. Nor would true pluralists want to blur the boundaries among the options for Jewish commitment. Like Hoffman, they would urge depth of substance—maximal learning, serious practice—on every one of those Jewish paths and call for mutual respect and cooperation among them. That, I take it, is what Schechter called the "sole true guide for the present and the future."[5]

CHAPTER 13

Reconstructing Belonging

Deborah Waxman

Deborah Waxman is a rabbi and is president and CEO of Reconstructing Judaism.

Rabbi Mordecai Kaplan, the founding thinker of Reconstructionism, was bad at mathematics—intentionally. He repeatedly tried to bend the poles of ethnicity and religion into a circle, and along the way he insisted that they (we) could be 100 percent Jewish and 100 percent American (or citizens of any other democratic country). While Kaplan's theories predate Mary Douglas's axes of identity, had he encountered them, he probably would have resisted their categorizations. Kaplan and his circle consistently strove for holism in their efforts to repair one of the major breaks that modernity wrought upon the Jewish people: the separation of "Jew" and "Jewishness" from the religion of Judaism.

Reconstructionism can be succinctly defined as understanding Judaism as "the evolving religious civilization" of the Jewish people.[1] In a Reconstructionist analysis, there have been only two constants across the millennia of Jewish history: first, the Jewish people, and second, change. Our ancestors adjusted unselfconsciously to nonstop change, both internal and external, and rationalized the creation of these adjustments as God's will.

This capacity for change, along with a tendency toward resilience, was essential to our survival. Take, as one example, the emergence of rabbinic Judaism following the cataclysmic destruction of the Second Temple and the sudden impossibility of the sacrificial system prescribed in the Torah. Over millennia, our forebears created tremendous religious and cultural richness and a wide range of theological views, ethics, folk customs, foodways, and more across diverse locations, expressed in distinct languages. Kaplan gathered all of these expressions of Jewish vitality into the embracing category of "civilization," creating a capacious response to questions of whether Judaism is a religion, culture, ethnicity, or people.

Kaplan argued that while modernity introduced disruption, we modern (and now postmodern) people can, unlike our predecessors, self-consciously implement change to recreate relevance for Judaism and ensure continuity. We must draw on our vast inheritance along with contemporary wisdom and practice, even from secular society, to advance the Jewish civilization and the Jewish people. Reconstructionism draws particularly on the methods, findings, and practice of rationalism, pragmatism, and democracy. Kaplan insisted that we must acknowledge the shattering of the premodern, supernatural authority that previously enabled rabbinic authorities to set boundaries and prescribe behavior; in our day, we must derive strength from religious, political, and cultural diversity and maximize that strength through pluralism.

To oversimplify tremendously, Kaplan and the circle gathered around him had two major preoccupations. They were deeply concerned about politics: how to harness nationalism, the major discourse of the nineteenth and early twentieth centuries, for Jewish purposes; how to foster good citizenship in Jews' home countries, in Palestine/Israel, and on the planet; how to infuse democracy into Jewish organizations and religious practice; and how to legitimate diverse Jewish practice (both religious and nonreligious) in communal life. They sought as well to create a modern approach to religion: setting aside supernaturalism; developing nonpersonal theology and liturgy; rejecting the idea of Jews as the chosen people; generating non-halachic modes of cultivating ethical behavior; and embracing art, music, and other aesthetic expressions in worship. Today, Reconstructionists continue these explorations in their contemporary expressions while also wrestling with changing theories and practices around constructions of identity, the implications of emerging scientific findings, and the tremendous impact of the digital era on individuals and society.

In a Reconstructionist approach, decisions are made and life is lived in consultation with community, both horizontal (those gathered around us) and vertical (those who came before us and those who will follow). Precedent is important but not binding—Kaplan famously declared that halachah "has a vote but not a veto"[2]—and value-based decision-making weighs a broad range of values from both Jewish and secular culture. And since the Jewish community must make space for all individuals in our complex, intersectional identities, the community itself will be continually remade.

Since the Reconstructionist movement was founded a century ago, we have experimented with ideas, practices, and institutions. In spite of our small size, Reconstructionist innovations have been widely adopted—from the bat mitzvah to the concept of Jewish peoplehood to the understanding that Jews who married non-Jews did not intend to exit the Jewish community (made into policy in 1968, for example, in the formal recognition of ambilineal descent for children of intermarriage) to an embrace of LGBTQ Jews as community members and leaders. These and other commitments were originally received as controversial and disruptive even as they were ultimately embraced—usually first by the Reform movement and then more widely. Our principled and affirmative approach demonstrates how Jewish life and the Jewish people can flourish in an open society.

Today, the Reconstructionist movement remains at the cutting edge in our insistence on abiding relationship across difference, especially around conversations about Israel and Palestine; our exploration of new expressions of community and how to make the richest possible connection between communal life "online" and "on land"; our repudiation of chosenness and our efforts to champion Jewish particularism without embracing chauvinism; and our robust commitment to democracy in Jewish practice and in the structure of our movement.

Of course Hoffman is correct that Kaplan made Jewish peoplehood the abiding concern of the Reconstructionist movement (what he and Douglas would categorize as "group"). The last decades have pushed us toward significant reconceptualization in order to meet the demands of our times. We reconceptualize first and foremost by shifting from Kaplan's focus on nouns (civilization, peoplehood) and adjectives (religious, evolving) to verbs. We emphasize agency, ownership, obligation, and action. This is why, in 2018, we chose "Reconstructing Judaism" as the new name for the central organization of the Reconstructionist movement. Reconstructing Judaism amplifies a Reconstructionist approach for the benefit of all Jews even as we continue to train Reconstructionist rabbis and foster communities organized on Reconstructionist principles.

North American Jewish life is shifting from an ethnic moment into a post-ethnic time. North American Jews, especially those who affiliate with non-Orthodox movements, are rapidly moving away from being a community of descent (defined by biology) to being a community of consent. Jews today have countless opportunities to seek meaning and define their identities. Anyone who identifies as a Jew today *chooses* to be Jewish, regardless of their parentage or background. Reconstructionists seek to demonstrate that being Jewish is not simply an end in and of itself, but rather a means to living a deeply interconnected life and to increasing wisdom and equity in the world. We choose to live Jewish lives because doing so helps us to live lives of meaning and connection to each other, Jews and non-Jews alike, and with all creation. At Reconstructing Judaism, we have shifted our attention from *being* Jewish, which is significantly a conversation about boundaries and authority, to encouraging *doing* Jewish, whether it is by observing Jewish law, sharing a Shabbat meal, joining a synagogue (Reconstructionist or otherwise), or building a new expression of community. *Doing* Jewish may mean studying text, learning Hebrew or Yiddish, or taking a course on our website, Ritualwell. It may mean immersing oneself in social action and ethically based political engagement or preparing meals according to eco-kashrut principles. We believe that it is only possible to live a fully Jewish life in community, and we aim to support each person in finding their individual path to a responsive community where they can contribute their gifts and be supported in their wholeness.

From an intentional, values-driven perspective, we are building on the long-standing Reconstructionist project of generating a sense of connection and mutual obligation for the Jewish people that is informed, but not constrained, by halachah—what early Reconstructionists sought when they articulated the concept of Jewish peoplehood as a *means* toward interconnected living, not an end. Where Kaplan theorized about Jewish organizational life on a grand scale, today, in the face of ever-increasing isolation and polarization fueled by radical individualism and the internet, we seek something more intimate. We look to reconstruct "belonging" for the twenty-first century. We continue the work of gathering together the fringes, bringing the margins to the center, with the full understanding that this repeated practice will transform us and that these transformations will ultimately strengthen us. Our contemporary justice commitments are around centering the voices and experiences of Jews of Color, nonbinary people, people from different socioeconomic classes, and people with different abilities and working to break down structures and systems that work against equity and inclusion.

As Reconstructionists committed to living at the intersection of Torah and the Jewish people, we bring this to life through the practice of a set of intentional commitments: encounter informed by curiosity; an interest in forming abiding relationships; the cultivation of capacity for discomfort; an insistence on maintaining community across difference based on shared fundamental values; the constant nurturing of *anavah* (humility) and *chesed* (loving-kindness); the willingness to do *t'shuvah* (repentance) and make *tikun* (repair) where necessary; and the readiness to change, individually and collectively. We do this in the service of bolstering Jewish and Jewish-adjacent individuals and seekers and drawing them into communities that can help them—help all of us—feel valued and cherished and whole. We do this to honor our ancestors, nurture ourselves, and offer support and encouragement for the next generation of Jews—and the people who love us—to seed and nurture their own visions of Jewish community.

CHAPTER 14

A View from Outside the Denominations

Daniel A. Judson

Daniel A. Judson is the provost of Hebrew College in Newton, Massachusetts.

In 1958, Congregation B'nai Jehuda, Kansas City's oldest congregation and a long-standing pillar of Reform Judaism, faced a crisis so severe it was forced to convene a special congregational committee. The issue was growth. But the problem that so vexed the congregation would be unheard-of today: their problem of growth was that they had too much of it. In 1957, the congregation had built a massive new synagogue with thirty-one schoolrooms to accommodate 794 students. One year after the building was finished, they had grown to 924 students. The congregation decided to take the unusual step of paying a group of young families $6,000 *not* to join B'nai Jehuda and, instead, start their own new Reform synagogue. Remarkably, B'nai Jehuda was not the only Reform synagogue to use this tactic. For example, Holy Blossom Temple, the leading Reform congregation in Toronto, loaned $25,000 to a group of families to start a new synagogue, Temple Sinai.[1] Postwar America saw a massive surge of new Conservative and Reform synagogues built. A front-page *New York Times* article in 1959 titled "Judaism on Rise in Suburbs" claimed that 125 new Reform and Conservative synagogues had been built in the New York City suburbs since the end of the war.[2]

It would be a vast understatement to say that we are in a different moment now. Rabbi Larry Hoffman writes, "Before you can get where you are going, you have to know where you come from, but also where you are now." The answer to the last question, "Where are you now?," is that we find ourselves in a substantially different Jewish world than the postwar synagogue boom of the 1950s or even Jewish life in the 1990s. Denominations are in decline, and although I am not a prophet, nothing in the religious zeitgeist would suggest that this trend will be reversed.

To take just one data point, when I arrived in the southern suburbs of Boston twenty-five years ago to lead a small Reform synagogue, the area had two Reform synagogues, four Conservative synagogues, and one small Orthodox synagogue. Twenty-five years later, three of the Conservative synagogues have merged to form one independent synagogue, one Conservative synagogue closed and reopened as an independent synagogue, and one Reform synagogue, as well as the Orthodox synagogue, have closed entirely. To sum up, seven denominational synagogues became two independent synagogues and one Reform synagogue. Moreover, even that one Reform synagogue now has a rabbi from the Hebrew College Rabbinical School, a pluralistic seminary.

The trend of declining denominationalism has been borne out by recent Jewish population studies, which show a waning number of denominational adherents.[3] Added to this was the 2022 closure of Hebrew Union College–Jewish Institute of Religion's rabbinical program at its original Cincinnati campus because of lack of students, further exemplifying the difficult state in which the movements find themselves. Denominations have been a fact of American Jewish life for 150 years. Why is this the moment when our denominational history seems to be ending?

Sociologist and theologian Peter L. Berger once quipped that "American Judaism spawned a collection of denominations with truly Protestant exuberance."[4] This is a good reminder that Jewish religious phenomena in the United States often reflect Protestant trends. And just as Jewish denominations took root following their Protestant neighbors, so too does the Jewish denominational decline follow Protestant trends. Mainline Protestant churches have been declining for decades, and despite some recent reports that this trend may have slightly reversed, they are still a far cry from the 1950s, when more than half of all people in the United States belonged to mainline Protestant denominations.[5]

Declining denominationalism thus needs to be seen as an American religious phenomenon and not just isolated to the Jewish community. Just as Christianity has seen a rise in nondenominational churches that eschew fine doctrinal distinctions, so too the doctrinal distinctions between the movements of Judaism seem far less significant now than in previous eras. The Conservative movement's turn to egalitarianism and its opening up to LGBTQ rabbis alongside the Reform movement's acceptance of Hebrew and ritual have shrunk the divide between the two major movements. Even in the Modern Orthodox world, there has been movement around these issues, as places like Yeshivat Maharat in New York City produce female rabbinic leadership. This is not to say, of course, that there are no differences, but in particular the distinctions between Reform, Reconstructionist, and Conservative Judaism have come to feel rather narrow, particularly in light of all of the resources and energy that these movements presently devote to maintaining their separate structures.

Hoffman ends his essay by noting that many contemporary Jews, from all denominations, are "suspicious of institutions, authorities, and traditions; and left dangling on our own, as a consequence. That leaves us feeling increasingly alone but searching for spiritual meaning and forcing religion to re-present itself." Hoffman has incisively judged the condition of our time. Contemporary Jews, particularly younger Jews, often are suspicious of institutions defined by denominations. I might suggest to some young Jews that their response might be to delve into traditional Jewish sources, with guidance. Organizations like Mechon Hadar, which encourages yeshiva-style learning of Jewish texts and law; Svara, "a traditionally radical yeshiva," which teaches Talmud in a queer framework; and even my own institution, the Hebrew College Rabbinical School, which centers the *beit midrash* (study hall) as the core part of rabbinic education, have all placed learning of traditional texts as central to Jewish life. But each of these institutions stands outside the denominational world, teaching Judaism without embracing a particular denominational framework. At Hebrew College, we emphasize giving our students the capacity and skills to read traditional Jewish sources while also giving them the freedom to interpret those sources from a variety of perspectives. Students build meaningful community around study even—or perhaps especially—with study partners who adhere to different worldviews.

Organizations like these, which reignite young Jews' interest in classical sources, are also handing younger Jews the keys to recreating Jewish institutions. Learning provides a kind of authority that permits change, along with the "re-presentation" of Judaism that Hoffman suggests we need. Ultimately, Jewish life outside the denominations provides possibilities to meet the challenges of where we are now to give us a clearer sense of where we are going.

Section 5

From Common Cold to Uncommon Healing

In the 1990s, when Jewish leaders began to decry intermarriage as the reason for Jewish demographic decline, Rabbi Larry Hoffman, ever the contrarian, argued that intermarriage was inevitable and, conceivably, an opportunity to attract new (and more committed) Jews. His first article on the subject, adapted and excerpted here, was published in the CCAR Journal *(1994). In it, Hoffman encouraged Reform Jews to embrace forms of spirituality long shunned by the highly rationalistic movement. The essays that follow reflect on Hoffman's response in light of recent demographic trends.*

Doubts about Jewish continuity are the common cold of the Jewish psyche. The current spate of alarms predicting an impending Jewish demise invokes a sense of déjà vu, but it demands our attention nonetheless, since last gasps are known only in retrospect, and there is always a chance that this particular case may be the single instance that matters . . . are we sick with a passing cold, or are we on the verge of terminal pneumonia? That is what, so far, no one has been able to decide.

Leading communal observers blame intermarriage and urge rabbis to "eschew indulgence" and "just say no." I suggest that just saying no has proven unproductive thus far, and there is no reason to believe that it will get us anywhere in the future.

My own claim, as a liturgist, is that despite new prayer books, Reform Jewish worship remains unspiritual, unmoving, and unimportant. Regarding our synagogue service as symptomatic, I conclude that American Jewry is indeed wheezing badly. It will be cured only because the physicians of its spiritual health stop pretending nothing is wrong and initiate a regimen of creative spiritual medication.

Many of us suffer from the sense that all is not right with ourselves and society. People want ritual that heals: heals the broken selves, heals the wound of broken communal connection, and promises healing in a world that can prove shattering.

We have thus come full circle. Jewish demographers have pointed to a communal common cold. We now find that the cold persists because of the absence of healing in our synagogue services: healing of self (spirituality) and healing of others (social justice). Worship has to heal once again; it must matter.

A call to "just say no" will only go so far. We can heal our common cold only by attending to the synagogue and its worship in the ways outlined above. Spirituality that heals the soul of inner pain, and justice that heals the world's shattered population, must be the message people get when they come to pray. Knowing that they are in a community that heals, they may yet carry us proudly into a new century of promise.

CHAPTER 15

Living at the Margins of Jewish Life

Shira I. Milgrom

Shira I. Milgrom is rabbi of Congregation Kol Ami in White Plains, New York.

Rabbi Larry Hoffman suggests that "Reform Jews have taken upon themselves the task of living at the very margins of Jewish life, which is to say, by living closest to the people at the point where the axes meet," near point zero. Hoffman has called out the reality as he sees it, unafraid to name the truth. Using Mary Douglas's two-dimensional axis of identity, he argues that Reform Jews are the least likely to abide by a set of rules and least likely to feel an obligation to other members of their group or tribe.

Reform Judaism has been the most daring movement of contemporary Jewish life, challenging the status quo, transforming and revitalizing prayer, redefining membership in the community (patrilineal descent, non-Jewish members of Jewish families) and Jewish personhood (full enfranchisement of women and LGBTQ+ individuals). The margins have been a place of vitality, creativity, and spiritual openness. Indeed, a member of my rabbinic class at Hebrew Union College–Jewish Institute of Religion chose an internship on skid row, noting that God was more present in the rawness of life there.

Yet, we cannot sustain Jewish life living near zero on the number line. This essay is an invitation to think about generating rubrics in which (Reform) Jews might locate ourselves, moving away from zero toward a stronger and more vital place. Though neither "group" nor "rules" have drawn Reform Jews in, there are other potential areas we might mine to generate a meaningful Jewish practice: relationships, narrative, and spiritual wisdom.

Let us start with *relationships*. Reform Jews score low on Douglas's "group" axis, that is, "accepting the responsibility entailed by a network of personal relationships." However, we might think about strengthening a commitment to a Jewish practice on a more intimate scale of personal relationships, rather than on the scale of a broader network or tribe. Human beings do not live well in isolation. We don't live well when our circle of concern ends with us. We need relationships; we need to love and to care. We understand that a relationship that does not make any claims on us is not a deep or serious relationship. Any worthwhile relationship—a child, a spouse, a close friend—makes claims on us and engenders obligation. One Jewish word for obligation is "mitzvah." We might nourish a practice of "mitzvah," of holy obligation, by connecting our most intimate and familial relationships with a Jewish practice.

Loving is hard. Loving takes commitment. Whether it is caring for our siblings, our children, our parents, our friends, or our life partners—real loving requires commitment. Every Friday night at our Shabbat table, my husband, David, sings to me in the words of our tradition using a melody he composed himself. There have been weeks when I felt ignored—weeks when David's work or our children's needs were more important to him than I was. And undoubtedly, there have been weeks when he felt the same. What if we were to wait until we both felt in perfect sync with one another? What if our tradition didn't have Friday night? If Judaism didn't mandate behaviors? If my husband's words were not a committed part of our Friday night? How often would we stop to sing of our love? At the Shabbat table, we also hold and bless our children; we welcome and embrace our friends.

No full relationship can grow without commitment. Being a Jew means being in relationship. Learning to love, and not only when we feel like it. Behaviors bring us back to ourselves. Brit—being in covenantal, faithful love—is to commit to something larger than myself, something beyond how I feel at this or that moment. In the religious vocabulary of Judaism, commitment translates as "mitzvah." Love is critical, but mitzvah-as-commitment brings us back when love falters.

We Reform Jews may score low on the "group" criterion. It may be difficult to convince ourselves that we owe responsibility to other members of the Jewish tribe; however, it should not be difficult to tap into the responsibility we feel to our most intimate relationships. Jewish practice is a way to strengthen and celebrate those relationships.

Another potential rubric for generating a meaningful Jewish practice is the power of the *narrative*. More Jews participate in a Passover seder—and observe a conscious Jewish practice for the days of Passover—than in any other event of the Jewish year. Why? Because the story makes sense; it is clear, and it is compelling. We define ourselves by this narrative. We believe that the arc of history indeed bends toward freedom. This story compels us because we want to have the courage, still, to stand up to tyrannies and to place our hope in this vision of liberation.

Finally, when it comes to defining meaningful Jewish practice, there is *spiritual wisdom*. Hoffman notes, "Most of us are . . . increasingly distrustful of rules and relationships . . . left dangling on our own . . . searching for spiritual meaning." It is to that nexus of rules and spiritual meaning that I would like to turn. Religions are spiritual alphabets. They give us a language with which to explore the spiritual dimensions of the universe and with which to sculpt the spiritual dimensions of our own lives. Though other religions undoubtedly share deep wisdom, each also offers its own unique way to mine and shape the spiritual life.

Judaism's uniqueness lies in its pairing of spiritual wisdom with behavior. There is no essential Jewish value that doesn't find its expression in a behavior, a practice, or a ritual. Historically, this system of behaviors evolved into its own independent structure, the Jewish legal framework known as halachah. It rests on the divine nature of revealed scripture (Torah) and on the authority of rabbis who, over the centuries, have interpreted and expanded the law according to an intricate and clearly articulated system of legal reasoning. Halachah stands on its own as the reason for Jewish practice and behavior and, indeed, as Hoffman writes, has both generated powerful allegiance to a religious practice and created strong bonds among its adherents.

For the Reform Jewish community, however, halachah has long ceased to be a generator of Jewish practice. As Hoffman writes, we are indeed "left dangling"—and not only because we are not compelled by this system of rules; we are also severed from Judaism's unique way. Hovering near point zero provides insufficient nourishment for Jewish life in the present and endangers the sustainability of Reform Jewish life for the future.

Hoffman writes, "Most of us are in quadrant four, increasingly distrustful of rules and relationships; suspicious of institutions, authorities, and traditions; and left dangling on our own, as a consequence. That leaves us feeling increasingly alone but searching for spiritual meaning."

We need to do better. The Jewish world—indeed, the global world—needs what Reform Judaism has to offer: a religious life that is creative, spontaneous, intellectually honest, spiritually open, and ethically driven. Connecting with spiritual wisdom may offer the richest potential for a framework for contemporary Jewish practice.

In this model, spiritual wisdom is connected to a foundational Jewish concept, which can in turn be actualized by "a way to walk the path," a basic religious practice. We would generate a model that has three steps:

1. Foundational Jewish concept
2. Spiritual/emotional wisdom connected to that Jewish concept
3. Basic religious practice that provides a way to actualize that wisdom

There are countless possibilities for concepts and practices that can be linked this way. Here is one example:

1. Jewish concept: *k'dushah*/holiness
2. Spiritual wisdom: nourishing a heart of gratitude and wonder
3. Religious practice: blessings of the senses

This approach seeks to create somewhat unexpected pairings between Jewish concepts and spiritual wisdom, then ground that wisdom in an essential Jewish teaching and suggest a Jewish religious practice to act upon that wisdom. It is a modest project that I look forward to exploring further; hopefully it will contribute to alleviate, at least in small measure, the crisis that Hoffman describes, by suggesting a renewed and reinvigorated spiritual framework for contemporary Jews.

CHAPTER 16

Finding God with Other People

Noa Kushner

Noa Kushner is a rabbi and founder of The Kitchen, a Jewish community in San Francisco.

I was teaching about the *Mishkan*, that holy place we were commanded to create in the wilderness, in the middle of nowhere, so that we might meet with god.[1] The rabbis have elaborate and far-reaching interpretations of how we found what we needed in order to create such a place.

One item in particular captures the attention: the thirty-two-cubit (approximately forty-eight-foot) cedar beam.

According to the story, the tree from which this wood was to be taken is planted hundreds of years earlier by Abraham, our first collective ancestor, and then harvested by his grandson Jacob, who then somehow sneaks it into Egypt, where it survives generations of our slavery so that his children's children can sneak it back out into freedom again.[2] In one scene, Jacob is begging and pleading with his sons to carry that beam with them, no matter what. "Someday you will be asked," Jacob says. "I probably won't even be with you any longer, but, I promise, someday God will ask you—or maybe God will ask your children—for this beam. It will be for nothing less than holding up a place where you can meet with God. Make sure you are ready. Make sure you have everything you need."

I was teaching this story to a group of parents in our school. The kids and parents like our school; it is a shabbat school, the parents and students learn together in families, and our educators are incredible. What's not to like? Still, one parent raised her hand. "My daughter wants to know why we come here," she asked. "What should I tell her?"

The daughter's question is *the* question; it is our question.

"Why?" comes in all kinds of flavors and forms, but regarding religion, it is surely propelled by a larger society that, at best, does not understand religion and, at worst, dismisses it as irrelevant or oppressive. "Why?" in our context most often insinuates a need for justification. Therefore, if we try to answer this "Why?" question on society's terms alone—that is, if we try to recategorize religion as appealing or resonant without demanding any change in perspective from the one who is asking the question—we have already lost the argument. Instead, we must fundamentally alter the very basis of the conversation. We have to address where the "Why?" is coming from.

In other words, whether the synagogue is relevant is not the question. The question is whether *our lives* are relevant and, if so, to what end. This is not my idea. It is surely from the tradition; Heschel said it emphatically and best most recently.[3]

But the act of questioning our very lives is counterintuitive, and little in our world supports it, and so we need to remind each other what the right question is, again and again.

Returning to the mother's question, I said, "I think you should tell your daughter that the reason we come here on shabbat and pray and learn together is because, someday, God is going to ask her and us to build something holy, some kind of a holy place where God can meet us in this world, and you want to make sure she is ready.

"I'm dead serious," I said. "That really is the only possible answer."

Why religion? *Why* synagogues, or whatever you want to call the communal project of finding god with other people? Why? So that when we are asked, we'll be ready. We will remember that we have what we need, just as our ancestors had that cedar beam.

When we started The Kitchen, a religious community in San Francisco, about ten years ago, the energy around nearby Silicon Valley felt positively messianic. Social media was going to connect the world, for the better. New companies had value statements like Google's "Don't be evil"—and we actually believed they *wouldn't* be evil. Unlike those on Wall Street, the tech guys (and they were, and still are, mainly guys) were, we believed, the good guys.

Religion here, by comparison, felt like a relic, something to be politely tolerated, not engaged seriously. Some of that bias was well founded. Religion was not compelling. Religious expression seemed almost uniformly out of step.

So, in 2011, our first move was to incorporate all kinds of innovation and creative design. Bad design seemed like an inadequate reason for someone to reject a rich vein of religious thinking and doing, and it was relatively easy to try and address. We worked and still work on the words we use, the colors, the rooms we inhabit, and the experience a person might have.

But the more we tried to redesign a holy place, the more humbled I became in the face of the elegant genius of a communal shabbat. It was almost unparalleled in its design, that is, in its ability to bring together a large group of people, each with different, profound needs. Unlike organizations that constantly had to make the case for their own necessity, ours had a number of intensely compelling entryways, all inherited: Someone might join us out of a need to be with other people or to teach their children what it means to be in a holy space. Someone might join us out of a need to respond communally to a political event, a moment in history, or in society. Someone might want to engage personally with a mythic narrative, the stories that literally shape us, torah. Someone might want to seek an experience of holiness or god, however they define it. And here I am only scratching the surface.

The longer we kept going, the more I understood that there were an increasing number of doors, each one more immediate and fundamental than the next. A person could be mourning, or sick or pregnant or in love, and somehow, all of these circumstances lent themselves to a need to be together on shabbat. We invented exactly zero of these doors, but they were all there, unlocked, ajar, as if waiting for these generations to find and go through them.

Eventually, realizing how many ways individuals have of approaching Jewish community and how many diverse needs it serves, we stopped trying to build doors for each and every one. Instead, we just worked to make our shabbat the most powerful and transcendent one it could be.

In other words, instead of molding shabbat in order to respond to the "Why?" question, we started instead with the premise that shabbat was essential, the beginning. Rather than questioning the necessity of shabbat or religion or the institutions that help us find god with other people, we tried to ask harder questions about the way we live the rest of our lives.

Of course, over the years, even with the best of intentions, we still often forget to ask the hard questions. During the week we are dragged into budgets and politics, ego contests, our vanities and fears, all of those things that insert and inflate themselves, as if they are real and very important.

The difference is that on shabbat, now that we have it—and have each other, and the experience of building a holy place again and again—we remember more easily: Eden is real. Sinai is real. The wandering takes a while, but there is a promised land. Now we remember: Jacob was right; God still asks us to build holy places, and so we must be ready, we must make sure we have everything we need. Now we remember, as if we were in a dream: slavery ends, and when it does, the seas part for us every single time.

CHAPTER 17

From Common Cold to Uncommon Pandemic

Jonathan D. Sarna

Jonathan D. Sarna is a professor of American Jewish History at Brandeis University.

Rabbi Larry Hoffman is an eminent scholar, teacher, and Jewish public intellectual. His writings have informed and enriched Jews of every type and have also influenced the field of religion as a whole. His generosity toward colleagues and students, as well as his *menschlichkeit*, are legendary. So it is an honor to respond to him—even years later and in respectful disagreement. This essay responds to the complete text of Hoffman's 1994 article, "From Common Cold to Uncommon Healing," where he makes a number of specific claims:

1. Every generation of American Jews has feared that it may be the last.
2. Intermarriage is inevitable in a free and open society and not worth fighting. Indeed, we may actually gain from adding converts to our ranks.
3. Synagogues fail to offer Jews the moral leadership that they crave.
4. Synagogues should focus on meeting the spiritual needs of American Jews and focus on healing; they should offer Jews "creative spiritual medication."

Let me address each of these claims in turn:

1. I totally agree with Hoffman that today's American Jews are, in philosopher Simon Rawidowicz's memorable term, an "ever-dying people."[1] Every generation has worried—with ample reason—that it will be the last. And every generation has "miraculously" gone on to produce another generation to worry anew. That, however, does not mean that we should dismiss this fear as our "common cold." Instead, we should appreciate it for what it is: a mortal fear of death. As such, it has served as an amazing motivator, stimulating innovation, revitalization, and the philanthropic generosity that has repeatedly managed to stave off what is described in the Yom Kippur liturgy as the "evil decree." Fear that Jewish life will not survive has, time and again, helped to ensure that it does.

2. At the time he wrote this essay in 1994, Hoffman presciently understood that intermarriage could not be prevented. Jews who sought to promote in-group marriage faced a cultural mainstream, including Jews, that legitimized and even celebrated the marry-whomever-you-fall-in-love-with ideal. As mixed marriages of every kind proliferated in the United States, crossing ethnic, religious, and racial lines, young people came to view opposition to intermarriage as un-American and racistly tribal. In Reform congregations, promoting endogamy became harder and harder.

   Hoffman, ever the optimist, hoped that non-Jews who married Jews might in time convert to Judaism. That did not much happen: conversion numbers have scarcely risen over the past decades. But, contrary to what many predicted, a plurality of the children of intermarried couples now proudly identify as Jews. That explains, in part, why Jews in 2020 number 7.5 million in America, up from fewer than 6 million when "From Common Cold to Uncommon Healing" first appeared.[2]

   Yet intermarriage has transformed American Jewish life more than anyone once thought possible. If anything, Hoffman's "common cold" grew into a pandemic. An astonishing 72 percent of non-Orthodox Jews who have married since 2010, according to the most recent Pew study, describe their spouses as being "non-Jewish" (in the 1990s, that number was closer to 41 percent). And on a host of core Jewish beliefs, a wide chasm now divides those married to non-Jews from those with Jewish spouses. Those with non-Jewish spouses report less sense of belonging to a wider Jewish community. They feel less responsibility than those married to Jews to help other Jews in need around the world. They express far less attachment to Israel. And when asked whether "it is very important that their grandchildren be Jewish," the vast majority say no.[3] There is nothing "common" about any of this. We ignore intermarriage's impact at our peril.

3. In the full 1994 article, Hoffman was way ahead of his time in arguing that "synagogues fail to offer Jews the moral leadership that they crave." Sitting at the very institution where Rabbi Stephen S. Wise once thundered for social justice, Hoffman understood better than some of his peers that moral leadership could engage those otherwise distanced from Jewish life. "We matter on earth because we can make life better for others," Hoffman declared. Many readers doubtless nodded in agreement.

   Hoffman could not have predicted the great moral lapses—revelations of sexual harassment and abuse—that would later be revealed across synagogue life, and within the Reform movement and Hebrew Union College–Jewish Institute of Religion in particular.[4] Moral leadership, we now understand, begins at home. Ethical engagement in the community must be reinforced by ethical behavior at home and in the synagogue. Rabbis must be "moral exemplars." They dare not preach what they themselves fail to practice.

   Beyond this, it seems to me that the complexity of ethical engagement demands more attention than Hoffman gives it here. Jewish teachings, for example, often conflict concerning knotty moral issues. Rabbinic views may also differ from contemporary liberal views concerning issues like marriage, childbearing, the centrality of Zion, and *ahavat Yisrael* (love and support of our fellow Jews). Moreover, as readers of the journal *First Things* know, ethical engagement among Christian thinkers has pushed in directions from which many liberal Jews would recoil. So, there is no simple recipe for providing Jews with "the moral leadership that they crave." Still, I agree with Hoffman that Jews ought to be able to look to their rabbis for moral guidance. More rabbis should provide it.

4. Hoffman's central point—that synagogues should focus more on spirituality and healing—may puzzle contemporary readers. Don't temples and synagogues already do that? What about "Mi She-beirach," Debbie Friedman's healing prayer, sung in synagogues across the nation? The answer, of course, is that, back in 1994, healing was still a new idea to rabbis, one that, in Reform Judaism, had most often been the domain of doctors and psychiatrists. Debbie Friedman composed her prayer seven years earlier, according to her friend Drorah Setel, writing in the *Forward*,[5] but it took time to spread from the margins to the mainstream and even more time to become part of a healing liturgy as important to many temple-goers as the Torah service itself.

Other Jewish spiritual movements, from Esther Jungreis's Hineni to the National Center for Jewish Healing, likewise turned to metaphors of illness in the late twentieth century. Minds, bodies, spirits, synagogues—all stood in dire need of medication, these spiritual diagnosticians proclaimed. Across the spectrum of Jewish life, rabbis heeded those prescriptions, adding emotive prayer, innovative rituals, song, dance, the embrace of community, and other spiritual and mystical elements to worship services that many felt had grown stuffy and stale.

Hoffman has good reason to take pride in his contribution to these developments. Yet I cannot but wonder if these new spiritual medicines of the 1990s have succeeded, as Hoffman projected, in carrying us "proudly into a new century of promise." The Reform movement today is smaller and poorer than when Hoffman's essay first appeared. Rabbi Lance Sussman, for one, admitted in a 2022 essay that Reform Judaism is "demographically challenged." It is likewise, he wrote, "challenged by a rising generation which is creating new and unprecedented expressions of Judaism outside the boundaries of congregational and denominational life. Affiliation is shrinking. Jewish identity and spirituality are morphing."[6] Instead of "uncommon healing," many American synagogues and temples find themselves far sicker than before.

Moral leadership and "creative spiritual medication," however necessary, are insufficient to meet the challenges facing twenty-first-century synagogues. The digital revolution, the vast impact of intermarriage, and over two years of pandemic-related disruptions and nightmares demonstrate that synagogues will need to do far more to win congregants back. As a starting point, the recent success of online Jewish learning initiatives and text-study programs of many sorts suggests to me that far more attention be paid to a term not found at all in Hoffman's article. The term is "Jewish education."

Section 6

Non-Jews and Jewish Liturgy

In 1978, Rabbi Alexander Schindler (1925–2000), second president of the Union of American Hebrew Congregations (today's Union for Reform Judaism), established Outreach, a program "aimed at all Americans who are unchurched and who are seeking religious meaning." This stemmed in part from an effort to reverse the age-old rejection of Jews who intermarry, promising instead to "draw them even closer to our hearts, to do everything we can to make certain that our grandchildren will nonetheless be Jews, that they will be part of our community and share the destiny of the Jewish people." A legal opinion authored by the Responsa Committee of the Central Conference of American Rabbis in 1969 urged congregations to attempt maximal inclusion. However, subsequent opinions of 1979 and 1983 were less inclusive. In 1989, Rabbi Larry Hoffman was asked to register his own opinion, as a liturgist, and it was published in the CCAR Journal. *An excerpt from that essay follows, along with two contemporary responses that demonstrate the ways in which the terms of the debate have shifted dramatically over the last thirty years, as communities have moved from language of permission and acceptability to acceptance and appreciation.*

The very idea that non-Jews would want to recite Jewish liturgy should not be taken lightly. It is a sign of how far we have come in the grand experiment of pluralism that may in the long run turn out to be North America's greatest contribution to human history.

The argument so far has depended on theological considerations and halachic (Jewish legal) guidance of Reform responsa and their precedents. But there is another kind of text here: liturgical texts—the prayers themselves, that is—which prompt the discussion in the first place. Even if the final halachic decision were to go against non-Jewish reading of all these liturgical texts, insofar as they constitute theological statements about *our* Shabbat, God's choosing *us*, and the like, it turns out that prayer is more than theology, and the act of worship more than the process of declaring one's faith in this or that doctrine. Prayers are not intended as essays for our leisurely rational consideration, which we then accept as true or reject as false. The prayer book is not a text to be studied; it is a ritual script to be played out.

The language of prayer is, therefore, only slightly informational. People engage in it not so much to tell truths as to perform tasks. Among other things, prayer creates community, marks sacred time, expresses thanksgiving, voices our deepest yearnings, tells sacred tales, affirms age-old hopes, assures us that life is meaningful, commits us to certain behavior, and orders our spiritual and ethical priorities. The question regarding non-Jews' participation in Jewish rituals is therefore only partly dependent on the "truths" that non-Jews may (hypothetically) say, or not say, with a clear conscience. More important are the "performative" meanings to the prayers in question, the tasks that the prayer is intended to perform.

Consider the ritual in which a Torah [scroll] is passed down through the generations. [Editors' note: This ritual has become standard practice at Sabbath morning services in liberal congregations to dramatize the coming of age of a bar/bat mitzvah.] There, it is the action, not the words, that speak loudest. I can imagine that some parents who raise their child as a Jew, despite their own non-Jewish status, might well want to participate in such a ceremony, not because their own heritage is being delivered to their child, but because the passing down of Torah affirms the Jewish tradition that they worked so hard to nurture in their offspring. If they wished to, why couldn't non-Jewish parents hand down the Torah scroll as a vivid symbol of the way they accepted Jewish tradition into their homes, inculcated it in their children, and now proudly watch those children accept the Torah as their lifelong spiritual guide?

The arguments from theology and from legal responsa should be supplemented with an understanding of how prayer functions, and that consideration has yet to become part of our conversation.

CHAPTER 18

Abraham or Ruth?

The Quest for Jewish Continuity

Joshua M. Davidson

Joshua M. Davidson is the senior rabbi at Congregation Emanu-El in New York City.

Ever since God commanded Abraham to sacrifice Isaac on Mount Moriah (Genesis 22), we Jews have worried about our survival. True, Abraham expresses no outward concern as he leads his son up the mountain. The same man who argues on behalf of the innocent people of Sodom and Gomorrah falls shockingly silent when it comes to his own son. But the commentaries do not mistake Abraham's silence for certitude. According to Rashi (Rabbi Solomon, son of Isaac, from eleventh-century France), Abraham is filled with doubt as he and Isaac make their ascent. Had not God promised him that his seed would be as numerous as the stars? Seeing the mountain in the distance, Abraham remarks to his servants, "We will see what will become of God's promise."[1]

From then until now, we have agonized over this question. Jewish continuity is important to us for many reasons. We Jews believe, not sanctimoniously but earnestly, that we have a story to tell and, with it, a set of values to share with the rest of humanity. We believe that if we live out that story and live by those values, we can have a positive bearing on the future of God's creation. Furthermore, we appreciate Judaism's power in our lives. It teaches us faith, and in faith we find hope. It offers us community, and in community we find strength. We want the next generation to have these too.

And Jewish continuity is important to us because no people wants to die. The philosopher Ahad Ha-Am (1856–1927) called this life force *cheifetz hakiyum*, the communal "will to survive."

So, how best to approach this challenge? The Bible suggests two paradigms: Abraham's and Ruth's. After the death of Sarah, Abraham sends his servant to find a "proper" wife for his son Isaac, ordering, "Swear by Adonai, the God of heaven and the God of the earth, that you will not take a wife for my son from the daughters of the Canaanites among whom I dwell" (Genesis 24:3). Abraham fears that if Isaac marries a Canaanite woman, she will seduce him into the worship of Canaanite gods, ending the Covenant with Abraham's God. So he dispatches his servant to find among his own extended family a woman predisposed to perpetuate the Covenant or, at the very least, one who bears no allegiance to the local gods. The servant encounters Rebecca and brings her home for Abraham's son.

Perhaps the writers of this story sought to impress upon their readers that the necessity of sustaining the Covenant between the people and their God demanded a rejection of intermarriage. And indeed I know that most intermarriages today reflect assimilation and often a drifting away from Jewish life. This has led some sociologists to warn that intermarriage poses the greatest threat to Jewish continuity. For three reasons, however, I reject that conclusion as unhelpful.

First, no public handwringing will change the reality of intermarriage, when so many societal guideposts already signal acceptance and approval.

Second, when we chastise Jews for intermarrying and portray those they love as risks to our community, we are alienating Jew and non-Jew alike.

Third, the greatest threat to Jewish continuity today actually lies in our failure to provide Jewish children with opportunities for Jewish engagement that demonstrate why their own children should be Jewish. At a time when continuity cannot be taken for granted, old educational approaches are inadequate. We need new ones to address new social realities.

Fortunately, the Hebrew Bible offers another story and paradigm for Jewish survival. Ruth was a Moabite woman who married an Israelite man and lived and worshipped with his family. After his death, she chose to become Jewish: "Your people shall be my people, and your God my God," she tells her mother-in-law, Naomi (Ruth 1:16).

Ruth should inspire us to embrace newcomers to our community, as well as to recognize the contribution of non-Jewish spouses who support their partners' Jewish lives (something Ruth was doing before her formal affirmation of faith) and non-Jewish parents who nonetheless are committed to creating Jewish homes and raising Jewish children. These precious individuals—precisely those Rabbi Larry Hoffman identifies in his essay—help us ensure Jewish continuity. And we as a community should find ways to celebrate them and thank them. It is compassionate and also beneficial for our future. When we count intermarried couples who have chosen to connect with Reform congregations, we discover that 98 percent of their children are being raised as Jews.[2] And when non-Jews express interest in joining our people though study and conversion, we must welcome them with open arms. We are a people that embraces newcomers. According to a midrash on the Book of Exodus, the Torah was given in the wilderness, a place that is open and accessible to all, so that everyone wishing to accept it could come and do so.[3] In our day, when individuals—including Jews—can either choose Judaism or reject it, Jewish survival depends on the extent of our welcome.

But the field of outreach never has been, nor should it be, directed only toward the non-Jews who might join or support us. While there are countless would-be Jews and encouraging spouses and parents standing tentatively at the threshold of the Jewish community leaning in, there are many more marginalized Jews whose entrance or exit will be determined by our efforts. Among them are increasing numbers who appear regularly on our doorsteps admitting a vague notion of their Jewishness but having little knowledge of how to begin to explore it.

No single path toward engagement will suffice. Everyone's journey is unique, determined not only by our starting point but also by our individual passions and interests, be they literature, history, visual arts, theater, music, or issues of national concern. Consequently, congregations can engage more people by opening multiple portals. We can offer new Jewish pathways to spiritual fulfillment by harnessing the exciting new currents of Jewish creativity already flowing largely outside our institutional walls. Communal life built exclusively around worship, study, and membership will not suffice if we want to connect with individuals on the Jewish periphery who may lack Jewish knowledge, experience, and institutional commitment and who often feel uncomfortable in the typical synagogue setting. Once they are in the door, of course, we may entice them with the beauty of Jewish ritual and the power of our textual tradition—encouraging them to reach for their next level of Jewish learning and living, whatever that may be.

In 1964, *Look* magazine ran a cover story titled "The Vanishing American Jew," which predicted that because no ethnic group had ever survived more than three generations in America, the Jewish community, too, would assimilate and vanish. We have fared far better than *Look* magazine—we have survived! Yet from Mount Moriah's peak, Abraham's question about our future still echoes down through the ages for every generation to answer: "What will become of God's promise?" he asks. How our children respond will depend on our choices and our commitments. As Leo Baeck, the philosopher and embodiment of Jewish continuity in the face of Nazi terror, once said, "Every generation by choosing its way ... chooses ... the way of its children."[4] Let our way be one of vibrant creativity, spirited commitment, and warm welcome.

CHAPTER 19

Where Tradition and Reality Collide
A Jewish Liturgy of Solidarity and Action

Hilly Haber

Hilly Haber is a rabbi and director of social justice organizing and education at Central Synagogue in New York City.

> Only a prayer that has its ear attached to the earth, its eye upon those who suffer, and its hands stretched out in solidarity can help us realize our distance from God and a world in flaming pain. If a prayer is about loving God, then prayer is also about building a house for the abandoned, becoming a wall of protection for the vulnerable, and giving our life away for those who are at the brink of disappearance.[1]
>
> —Claudio Carvalhaes, *Liturgies from Below:*
> *Praying with People at the End of the World*

In 2018 and 2019, a diverse group of over one hundred Christian scholars, clergy, and activists traveled to four different countries to pray with communities gripped by poverty, climate change, and war, with the purpose of creating liturgy for Christians around the world.[2] Sponsored by the Council for World Mission, their work is captured in the theologian and liturgist Claudio Carvalhaes's *Liturgies from Below: Praying with People at the End of the World*, a volume comprising prayers, poetry, and commentaries that draw on the lived experiences of oppressed and marginalized people as their primary sources of liturgical and theological knowledge. The resulting texts communicate the stunning hope and resilience of people living in a world on fire and a warning to those on the pulpit who would turn a blind eye to the flames. Take, for example, the poem "Worship Spaces in the Philippines," which opens:

> *In the space between pulpit and pews*
> *There's a sermon*
> *There's a baby crying of hunger*
> *And plenty rushing to calm her*
> *Before the need to be fed*
> *Becomes the only message heard*[3]

In this author's words, "the space between pulpit and pews," the gap between sacred text and lived experience is opened up and plumbed, sanctified and set apart as its own source of liturgical knowledge. The sermon takes place where tradition and harsh reality collide.

Rabbi Larry Hoffman's essay takes place in the same space between pulpit and pew. Citing the example of a non-Jewish parent who facilitates his or her child's Jewish education but is not counted as a link in the chain of Jewish tradition, Hoffman raises the question of whether, perhaps, rather than contorting reality to fit Jewish custom, Jewish ritual and prayer should instead reflect and comport with lived experiences within Jewish communities.

What is at stake in this distinction? In *Secular Ritual*, anthropologists Sally F. Moore and Barbara G. Meyerhoff underscore the danger that can result from the tension between ancient ritual and modern life: "Underlying all rituals is an ultimate danger, lurking beneath the smallest and largest of them, the more banal and the most ambitious—the possibility that we will encounter ourselves making up our conceptions of the world, society, our very selves."[4] When ritual performances feel dissonant from the realities of our identities and experiences, they run the risk of becoming irrelevant or, worse, dishonest.

In exposing the potential gap between the function and meaning of prayer and its legal and traditional uses, Hoffman points toward a new methodology for creating and performing Jewish worship, one that takes lived experience and context into account. What begins for Hoffman as a history lesson on inclusion and outreach within the Jewish community concludes with the foundational questions underlying the participation of non-Jews in Jewish life-cycle events, namely: What are the sources of our theological and liturgical knowledge? How do we speak about and with God? How does identity shape and inform the content and meaning of worship? Hoffman introduces the possibility that Jewish law and tradition need not have the last word on questions of participation and inclusion, and thus our prayers can better reflect the lived experiences of worshippers.

Taking lived experience as his own starting point for liturgical knowledge, Carvalhaes offers another paradigm. Beyond being simply a collection of prayers, *Liturgies from Below* exemplifies a methodology, a path toward creating liturgical resources with and from particular communities that resonate universally and speak to a world in crisis. Informed by tradition and scripture and born on the front lines of injustice, the poems, prayers, and rituals contained in this volume call us toward individual and collective transformation. As Carvalhaes writes:

> Through our collective prayers, with those who we are called to listen to, serve, and fight for, God calls us to live our faith in much deeper ways, understand our world in broader ways, and make a radical commitment with the poor in the name of God. Through prayers, we can envision a radical moral imagination of new worlds! By the grace of God, we can birth these new worlds through *ora et labora*—our prayers and our work in solidarity.[5]

Listening to and amplifying the voices of those on the margins, paired with ritual performance, allow us to imagine a world healed and to dedicate ourselves to making it real.

What new possibilities emerge for Jewish liturgy and theology when we look not only to our ancient texts for theological knowledge, but also to our individual and collective realities as a way of accessing eternal truths and meaningful worship? In introducing the possibility that Jewish law need not have the final word on the scope and boundaries of Jewish rituals, Hoffman points toward a Jewish methodology for creating liturgies from the place where the pulpit and the world collide, prayers and rituals that would speak to the world inside and beyond the walls of the synagogue. What would it look like for a group of Jewish clergy, scholars, and lay leaders to pray with people in prisons, people seeking refuge in new countries, people who have lost their homes to natural disasters, and to reimagine or create Jewish liturgies based on their experiences, liturgies that raised the voices of those on the margins and called the congregation to action?

As Rabbi Abraham Joshua Heschel wrote, "The moment we become oblivious to ultimate questions, religion becomes irrelevant, and its crisis sets in. . . . Religious truth does not shine in a vacuum."[6] As we draw from the deep wells of our heritage, let us also look to the landscapes of our local and global communities and allow our tradition to heal this broken world.

Section 7

The Jewish Leader You Want (or Want to Be)

In 2006, through the generosity of Bonnie Tisch, Rabbi Larry Hoffman began the Bonnie and Daniel Tisch Fellowship Program, a cocurricular program at the New York campus of Hebrew Union College–Jewish Institute of Religion, to impart his not-so-obvious recipe for clergy excellence. This essay, intended to inspire students and recruit them to the fellowship, sums up his criteria for outstanding Jewish leadership. It is followed by two essays by Tisch Fellowship alumni describing their recipe for Jewish leadership in the twenty-first century.

I define leadership in terms of three short mandates: (1) speak differently, think "bigly"; (2) demand honesty and excellence; (3) pursue depth: intellectual, artistic, and emotional.

(1) Speak differently, think bigly. Speaking differently is critical. Knowledge happens when we find the right words to express it. If you cannot speak it, you do not yet fully know it.

People also think that we convince others by arguing better, but philosopher Richard Rorty observes that progress comes not by "arguing well" but by "speaking differently."[1] Most people whom you try to convince are probably used to the usual arguments, which have not convinced them so far and probably won't this time either. Speaking differently, however, presents your case anew, in language for which the listener is unprepared, language they might listen to and become interested in.

Think of religion as *the practice of communicating in a register that does justice to the human condition.* Part of that condition includes ordinary things like eating, working, and so on, but religions harbor centuries-long conversations on ultimate things as well: Why are we born? What happens when we die? What makes us worthy of life? What is life's purpose? In our culture, however, we're not used to talking about these matters, so Jewish leaders need to learn how to do it. Jewish leaders go beyond the bromides and encourage creative and exciting ways to think anew about these ultimates.

The ungrammatical "think bigly" is an instance of speaking differently: the two ideas go together. If religions did not inherently think bigly by speaking differently, we would not need them. Communities require a non-judgmental setting where people are not afraid to float big ideas and to risk being wrong, not just about ultimates, but about everyday issues too.

(2) Demand honesty and excellence. The universe naturally tends toward the randomized meaninglessness that we call "entropy": things falling apart, running down, and wearing out; important papers out of place, lost emails, and accidental misunderstandings, not to mention random disease, early death, and our best efforts gone awry. The human condition regularly faces the threat of entropy, so it generates a *human project*: to construct a life of pattern, meaning, love, and hope, especially when entropy threatens us with their loss. Mediocrity is to the human condition what entropy is to the universe as a whole. As the universe trends toward entropy, so human nature trends toward mediocrity.

Jewish leaders are trained within organizational structures that are especially prone to bureaucratic mediocrity. They conveniently delude themselves into thinking that because the institution is good for them, it is objectively good for everybody, and, therefore, "excellent." Self-delusion is our greatest enemy. Only rigorous honesty can overcome this default position of satisfied self-centeredness. When critiques born of honesty are allied with thinking bigly and speaking differently, visions of excellence follow. Speaking differently offsets echo-chamber mediocrity and delivers creative excellence instead.

(3) Pursue depth: intellectual, artistic, and emotional. The opposite of mediocrity is excellence; the opposite of self-delusion is honesty. Mediocrity and self-delusion foster superficiality, the opposite of which is depth.

Mediocrity + self-delusion = superficiality
Excellence + honesty = depth

Jewish organizations understand the need to represent the spiritual, the moral, and the relational (our relationship with God and with one another), but they rarely represent them deeply. It is easier to mouth truisms, to traffic in banality, than to speak differently and think bigly. As with everything else, only speaking differently and thinking bigly rescue us from superficiality. "Spirituality" and "relationships," for example, have become banalities. Mouthing them as truisms is not enough; they must be rooted in intellectual, artistic, and emotional depth.

CHAPTER 20

Speaking Differently

Visible Voices

Sarah Grabiner

Sarah Grabiner is a cantor and the assistant director of the Year in Israel Program at Hebrew Union College-Jewish Institute of Religion in Jerusalem.

I have a visceral memory of sitting in a Brooklyn synagogue late on a Saturday night at a S'lichot service, preparing for the High Holidays. We were about to sing the evocative, challenging confession as a community for the first time that year: "*Ashamnu, bagadnu, gazalnu . . .*" ("We have trespassed, we have betrayed, we have stolen . . .").

Before we all rose, Rabbi Rachel Timoner spoke about the tradition of beating one's chest during this recitation, which I had witnessed and performed so many times. If you beat your chest at every confession at every service, your body can feel black and blue by the end of the season of repentance. It is not a gentle aspect of our tradition. Yet, something different about her words changed how I would consider that action forever.

Rabbi Timoner spoke of how little she connected to the notion of hurting oneself, even figuratively, as an act of ritual. Without jettisoning the custom altogether, she offered a reinterpretation: this was not a time of punishment; the focus should be not on wrongdoing, but on radical opening up, an opportunity for unfurling the layers under which we had been hiding. Rather than beating our chests to hurt ourselves, she spoke of this gesture as an attempt to tear through the toughened, coarse exterior, to symbolically break through the stories we tell ourselves and others to cover up our vulnerabilities to get to our core, our heart, and its yearnings, struggles, and hopes.

Her message is for me a wonderful example of the type of "speaking differently" that Rabbi Larry Hoffman would have us do in order to "think bigly" for ourselves and our congregations. The very order of his two processes, speaking and then thinking, is itself fascinating, because we might assume that it would be better to first sit and think before we attempt to speak publicly, emphatically, and impactfully. That is certainly the message of Robert Grosseteste's thirteenth-century maxim "Who thinks well speaks well."[1] Yet Hoffman invites us to consider speaking not as the outcome of thinking, but rather as part of its formative process. And not just any speech, but speech that is somehow different. Only when we craft our ideas into utterances in new and unusual ways can we achieve the strange yet alluring goal of "thinking bigly."

How public should this process be? Should leaders first prepare privately with a "speaking differently" phase before a public declaration? Or should different speech be part of communal life? Hoffman writes that speaking differently characterizes good religious leadership, "communicating in a register that does justice to the human condition." For this to be true, leaders should speak differently not only when sitting in their offices honing sermons or turning phrases over to perfect an article. Speaking differently, while scary and risky, should characterize our public Jewish discourse.

What, I wonder, does speaking differently actually sound like? I felt the impact of that kind of speech during S'lichot that night in Brooklyn, but it is difficult to put my finger on why Rabbi Timoner's words had such a transformative impact on me. What about them was "different"? If you are looking for a step-by-step guide to speaking differently and thinking "bigly," I am afraid that neither I nor, I believe, Hoffman has the answer. I instead invite you to reflect on a time when you might have encountered this phenomenon yourself. Using words, Rabbi Timoner took an action that I had previously experienced as punitive and harsh and turned it into an act of self-exploration, of burrowing deeper inside our souls and breaking down the thick outer layers that daily coat our hearts, to discover the essential. Even if I cannot quite tell you how, she spoke differently, and following her lead, I was able to think more "bigly" about this action and its meaning than I could have imagined.

What might we learn from our sacred tradition about how to speak differently? In fact, speaking differently is a divine trait; when God practices speaking differently before the entire community, the results can be transformative, indeed revelatory. While we read much in Torah about Moses's encounters with God, there are but a few descriptions of democratic experiences of the Divine. However, at Mount Sinai, we are told, all of Israel experienced Revelation together: "All the people were seeing the voices and the flashes and the call of the shofar and the mountain smoking" (Exodus 20:15).[2]

A midrash emphasizes the strangeness of this description: the people saw that which is usually heard.[3] Somehow, God spoke differently, articulating this moment of Revelation so that God's voice would be experienced unusually, with a whole host of senses. How can words be seen? How can more of our senses be brought into the communicative process? How embodied and immersive can language be?

Throughout our tradition, Jewish texts share ways in which divine speech is fundamentally different. As well as speaking in a visible voice, God utters multiplicities in a singular instant. Just before all the people saw God's voice, Moses heard God speak the Ten Commandments. Another midrash from the same collection tells us that God spoke all the commandments in one utterance.[4] We also encounter God's multifaceted speech in our Friday night Shabbat liturgy, in the first verse of the poem-hymn *L'cha Dodi*, which reminds us that God uttered "'keep' and 'remember' in a single word." This refers to the two versions of the Ten Commandments found in the Torah, one instructing us to "keep [*shamor*] the Sabbath" (Deuteronomy 5:12), the other to "remember [*zachor*] the Sabbath" (Exodus 20:8). For the rabbis of antiquity, these two versions of the commandment seemed to pose an existential threat: how could the Torah be inconsistent? Unless, that is, you take into account that God speaks differently. The midrash goes on to explain[5] that there is no contradiction between these two verses, since God spoke both words, *shamor* and *zachor*, in "a single word," as we recall each week in L'cha Dodi.

Not only does God speak a single yet divergent utterance, but that utterance is in every language at the same time! When the children of

Israel are standing at Mount Sinai, God speaks in "a great voice that did not increase" (Deuteronomy 5:19), a phrase that is difficult to parse and understand. The medieval French commentator Rashi interpreted "did not increase" as "it did not stop or cease, namely, God never had to stop speaking, even, for example, to breathe." The contemporaneous Spanish commentator Ibn Ezra, on the other hand, understood the phrase as meaning "it did not go on, namely it happened only once, and everything was communicated in one instant." Nothing is added or appended to God's great singular voice, which is heard in one long instant, and somehow everything is understood. Even more amazingly, in a midrash on this phrase, the early Talmudic sage Rabbi Yochanan proposes that God's one voice actually split into seven voices, which in turn split into seventy languages.[6] To the rabbis of antiquity, seventy languages might well have represented every imaginable people, nation, and way to communicate.

It was also divine creative words that brought the universe into existence: "May there be light ... sky ... water. ... And there was light ... sky ... water" (Genesis 1). Rabbinic tradition refers to God as "the One Who Spoke and the Universe Came to Be," describing how God speaks differently in the most "bigly," creative way we can imagine. Our own words might not have God's power of genesis, but they do have the power of metamorphosis. We know that our speech has the creative potential to inspire movements, build relationships, and transform communities. If even everyday words are powerful, what might different speech, the kind of speech that touches on the heart of human existence, be able to achieve?

If I dig deep to understand the impact of Rabbi Timoner's brief words, I see that her speaking differently changed the fundamental meaning of something for me that I had previously thought I understood. I thought I knew why Jews beat their chests on the High Holidays. I thought I understood the meaning of *t'shuvah* (repentance) and *cheshbon hanefesh* (accounting of the soul). But the way she used speech changed the entire framework of the High Holidays for me. Her words performed a real-world function: they prompted material change. Speaking differently might not always be about the exact words you choose; I had probably heard many of Rabbi Timoner's words before. Rather, what was different was the way in which her words made something happen; the way in which they played with sound and reference, embodiment and intellect, how they matched the mood and energy of the room, how they matched what was called for in that moment.

If religion, as Hoffman writes, is about "communicating in a register that does justice to the human condition," then the role of religious leaders is to hone the language that can perform this lofty, godly task: to speak differently. To make the world a different, better, more whole place because of our speech. I am, even in some small way, different because of how Rabbi Timoner spoke that night. How are you changed because of the different speech you once heard? How has your speech made even one person's world different? We cannot speak like God, making our voices visible, merging words, or communicating in multiple languages with a single utterance. However, Hoffman's words invite us to consider how we, like the Divine, can speak differently in order to think "bigly" and encourage those who listen to find creative and exciting ways to think anew.

CHAPTER 21

Artists of the Jewish Message

Joshua I. Beraha

Joshua I. Beraha is an associate rabbi at Temple Micah in Washington, DC.

Rabbi Larry Hoffman designed the Tisch Fellowship Program to inspire future clergy to see themselves as artists of the Jewish message, to speak differently, think "bigly," demand honesty and excellence, and pursue depth. What do Hoffman's suggestions look like in practice?

How can Jewish leaders speak differently and think "bigly"? How do Jewish leaders create cultures in which honesty and excellence thrive? How should Jewish leaders pursue depth?

1. **Speak differently, think "bigly."** Using new language and sentence constructions, from hallway conversations to our sanctuaries of worship, Jewish leaders today can speak into existence a fresh and inspired narrative, grounded in the past but with a new aesthetic, and new, imaginatively developed rationales for Jewish living that speak to the current moment. To write this new story, venturesome leaders will lead the way—akin to the authors of the Mishnah or the early Zionists, who, out of active faith and true desperation, came together from disparate parts of the world to generate a new form of Jewish life.

   The means by which to speak differently are as follows: read voraciously, do not blindly accept the given wisdom and language of the day, and speak from the particular.

   Problematically, twenty-first-century rabbis are better equipped to officiate at life-cycle rituals, lead prayers for healing, attend board meetings, argue on social media, and coordinate programs than they are to engage in scholarly conversations with wit and worldliness that transcend conventional thinking. To create new conversations, Jewish leaders in search of new language ought to open books—Jewish and not—engage with its content, ask questions of the text, and ultimately create for themselves a sustained practice of critical reading.

But new sentences and big ideas start small (as in the two-word construction "think bigly"). Despite American liberal Jews' enthrallment with universal and personal autonomy, Jewish thought has always arrived at the universal through the particular and found its strength within a shared communal system. Our ability to talk "in a register that does justice to the human condition," therefore, will be greatly strengthened if we can speak to it from the subjectivity of the particular.

2. **Demand honesty and excellence.** To arrive at the kind of rigorous honesty that Hoffman counsels, Jewish leaders must become scholars and champions of nuance and complexity. Ideological rigidity and one-sided thinking hinder a Jewish leader's integrity and their ability to see beyond themselves. After all, the fundamental purpose of Jewish study and living has always been to glean different approaches on a matter and to sift through partial truths.

The idea that Jewish thought values diversity of opinion is often celebrated and preached from pulpits countrywide but is rarely followed, especially as liberal Jewish leaders eagerly play into the cultural wars that are the perfect example of ideological inflexibility today. To foster the kind of honesty and excellence that might overcome bureaucratic mediocrity, Jewish leaders cannot remain blindly fixed in their core beliefs, for this further pushes them away from being trusted leaders outside of their own narrow tribal communities. True honesty in Jewish thought that serves to move the human project forward means admitting that a coherent whole is made up of multiple truths.

3. **Pursue depth: intellectual, artistic, and emotional.** Hoffman recognizes that "we have spent a generation emphasizing spiritual self-help, healing and wholeness, but at the cost of great ideas

about why Judaism matters in the first place."[1] Why Judaism matters first and foremost is that it upholds the idea of human dignity and freedom for all, which were known to the founders of the United States as "inalienable rights." But, today, liberal Jewish discourse fails to defend the infinite worth of the human being, what Alan L. Mittleman calls "that first-person point of view in which we recognize ourselves as unique, valuable, self-aware, and... self-determining moral agents."[2] Whether this failure is the result of consumer culture, the wellness industry, or our community's near-complete acculturation into an American society that has forgotten its spiritual connections to the Hebrew Bible, it is an inescapable fact that amid increasing moral chaos, the Jewish conversation has veered from its foundational principles and does not speak to its fullest potential for why the human project matters. In such a splintered political and cultural climate, Jewish leaders, like great artists, have an obligation to rise above the fray and to preach this universal message about human nature. In doing so, we will discover ways of being in the world, along with new rituals, that move us beyond the dull platitudes that currently guide us.

Greater depth can also be achieved by looking beyond our own self-interests. Historically—and possibly out of necessity—Jewish leaders have worked to preserve their institutions for the sake of the institutions themselves, but we live in a time incomparable to previous chapters in Jewish history. To further deepen the character of our communities, and our own selves, Jewish leaders can turn outward, toward the public square and the wider community. Assuming a posture that sees our communities as inextricably linked to a broader network of people and ideas will strengthen our capacity to deepen our own understanding of who we are and what we might uniquely bring to society.

Taken to heart, Hoffman's tenets ask Jewish leaders to become artists of the Jewish message. It is artists who are uniquely situated to pierce institutions prone to mediocrity. It is artists who can initiate pathbreaking ways of speaking and foster the conditions through which we might arrive at sincere and admirable new directions forward. It is an artist, like Hoffman himself, who can inspire generations of leaders to paint a new portrait of American Judaism—full of color, life, and depth.

Part 3

Jewish Behavior and Belief

Section 8

Text and Context

This essay epitomizes both Rabbi Larry Hoffman's unquenchable curiosity and his lifelong interest in cultural anthropology. Trained as a philologist, a student of texts and their transmission, Hoffman's first book was a study of the historical origins of the Jewish prayer book, The Canonization of the Synagogue Service *(1979). Soon, however, he reoriented himself from prayer texts toward the people who utter them and the rituals they enact, inspired by the anthropologists Clifford Geertz and Mary Douglas. This essay encapsulates what drew Hoffman to anthropology: his desire to go "beyond the text," a pithy phrase that served as title of his second book (1989). The three responses pick up where Hoffman left off, going beyond the text to explore questions related to the human body, linguistics, and theology.*

What is Judaism? Books? Even books catalogued neatly into piles? Or are the books really voices from the past that carry us to the Judaism of the present of which they speak? The old model of study, studying texts, is necessary insofar as we must determine the origin of the printed message before us. We must go beyond the text, to learn to ask new questions designed to unravel the inner world of the Jewish people out of which the messages emerge. This requires a much broader perspective than we have demanded, for which the best models of inquiry may be the humanities that study not books but people and societies. Today's agenda takes us from the texts to the living people who wrote them.

Writing about the customs of young French boys or Berber tribesmen, the anthropologist Clifford Geertz wrote, "The thing to ask. . .is not what their ontological status is [not just 'what they are,' that is]. . . . The thing to ask is what their import is: what it is, ridicule or challenge, irony or anger, snobbery or pride, that, in their occurrence and through their agency, is getting said."[1]

The same goes for a prayer. Unless we know the cultural significance of "what is getting said" when we pray, we flatter ourselves by thinking we know anything at all of liturgical importance. Sometimes people just mumble their way through a prayer. Sometimes, they make solemn promises; sometimes they are taken up short by a word or phrase that changes their lives; sometimes they do not care what the words say, but the music means the world to them. Studying the prayer book alone, as a text, is rather useless unless we begin accompanying it by asking people why they pray in the first place.

CHAPTER 22

What Will "Jew" Be?

Delphine Horvilleur

Delphine Horvilleur is a rabbi in Paris and editorial director of the quarterly Jewish magazine Tenou'a.

I clearly remember the day Rabbi Larry Hoffman invited us, his students, to play a game I would never forget. As we entered his classroom on the New York campus of Hebrew Union College–Jewish Institute of Religion, he simply wrote on the whiteboard four letters: P-A-I-N.

Then, he asked us how we would represent those four letters using only body movements. And there we were, twenty-five students in our twenties and thirties, in a liturgy class, playfully engaging in a mime game.

Someone started to move, demonstrating with clear talent what seemed to be "suffering." We were aching with him, watching the contortions of his hands and the hollow lines on his forehead. Some people started to laugh, as we often tend to do in these uncomfortable situations. Others clearly started to wonder what the "liturgical" meaning of this funny exercise was.

After a few minutes, Hoffman turned to me and said, "What about you, Delphine?" I immediately understood what he expected from me. And, slowly, I started to chew with appetite, pretending I was enjoying a snack: savoring a sandwich, most probably half a baguette filled with butter and Camembert.

As the only French student in the class (and actually in our entire New York seminary), I had a reading of those simple four letters that led me to a different interpretation from that of the English speakers around me. Because in French, the letters P-A-I-N mean "bread." And there I was, bringing a Parisian boulangerie's delicacy to our Manhattan conversation.

Suddenly, for all of us, everything became clear, and we all knew what the lesson was about.

With four letters and a few body movements, we were reminded that meaning is a matter of language, history, time, and space. It is an existential experience that relies upon a context. This anchoring creates an unbridgeable gap between the author and the reader, the speaker and the hearer, the text and the eye that perceives it. Letters, words, and sentences are brought to life by minds and bodies that come forth with their own experiences, origins, and unique translations.

This mime game we played clearly translated a profound liturgical truth that Hoffman kept teaching us, the same idea that lies at the core of his essay above: "Unless we know the cultural significance of 'what is getting said' when we pray, we flatter ourselves by thinking we know anything at all of liturgical importance."

The honest reader is therefore always invited to humbly experience the limitation of their grasp. Our reading is limited by the frontiers of our time, space, and bodies and requires us to acknowledge those restrictions. When we encounter a particular Jewish liturgical text, we need to realize that its writer used a language loaded with their own unique experience, which will always be partly eclipsed from the reader's mind.

And this recognition is at the core of the sacred art of interpretation. Interpreting liturgy is always an activity of investigation and a recognition of unavoidable misreadings and misunderstandings. We could call it the art of engaging in a "lost-in-translation" exercise. Reading can never be faithful, because only the writer (and maybe not even the writer!) can read what was meant to be read. The text will always mean more and less than it meant to its creator.

Liturgical pieces are intended to travel through time and to remain relevant for new generations. Words are kept as "sacred," but their sacredness never relies upon their absolute stability as much as it relies upon their unstable meaning. Their sacredness is only guaranteed by their relevance through time, which requires a constant reinterpretation in a new context. For the words of our liturgy to remain relevant, we attempt not only to understand their history and context, but also to engage in dialogue with a counterforce: the necessary unfaithfulness, in a new context, to an original meaning.

To say it more clearly, and using our mime game in Hoffman's classroom: the liturgist's "pain" might become "bread," a source of nourishment. Conversely, what profoundly fed the liturgist's mind or religious experience might become my generation's pain.

This recognition of a complex dialogue between generations and between cultures also applies to our identities. There is no such thing as a singular "Jewish identity," disconnected from space, time, body, and language. Our Jewishness is spoken through the unique language of our history, geography, or geology, stratified by different layers of our life experience.

Years ago, before I entered rabbinical school, in another stratum of my life, I was a medical student. In biology classes, I heard for the first time about epigenetics, the study of how our behaviors and environment can cause changes that affect the way our genes work. Scientists recognize today that our genomic expression—the way our bodies read our genetic sequence and act upon it—is largely dependent upon our environmental exposures. Therefore, with the very same DNA, identical twin brothers will evolve in different directions depending on the weather, their diet, historical context, or even the language they are exposed to.

What is true in biology is also true in religious thought and in identity building.

Our Jewish identity depends not only on the "genes" we inherit, but also on the environment in which we find ourselves. To become the commentator he is known as today, Rashi had to be French in the Crusaders' eleventh century. For Maimonides to become such an influential philosopher, he had to encounter Islamic thought, and Martin Buber developed his theology thanks to the twin influences of the Haskalah (Jewish Enlightenment) and Chasidism (Eastern European Jewish religious revival). Indeed, they, and we, are each the "authentic" Jews our encounters with otherness enabled.

My own "epigenetic" Jewish identity was irrevocably shaped by my French Jewish experience, and my exposure to other Jewish expressions influenced my reading, my interpretation, and my rabbinic path.

When people claim they understand what a text truly means or what a prayer says, they fail to see the limitations of their own grasp—just as my fellow students in that long-ago class with Hoffman believed there was only one way to interpret P-A-I-N. Just as we never precisely know what a text meant originally, we never know for sure what being a Jew meant at the beginning nor what it will mean one day in the future. And so we are left wondering and asking ourselves and the next generation, "What will 'Jew' be, when you grow up?"

CHAPTER 23

A Foot in Each Camp
Pushing the Boundaries of Both
Tony Bayfield

Tony Bayfield is a rabbi and former head of the Movement for Reform Judaism in Britain, and is professor emeritus of Jewish theology and thought at Leo Baeck College.

My respect and affection for Rabbi Larry Hoffman goes back so far that English law would use the phrase "since time immemorial." His approach to Judaism begins, for me, with an essay in *Beyond the Text* (1989) in which he draws on anthropology to introduce Judaism to the concept of liminality, a term that comes from the Latin word *limen*, "threshold," the doorway between inside and outside, the edge or margin between two ways of being. The festival of Sukkot straddles a liminal time in the Jewish year. The richly decorated sukkah celebrates a season of mellow fruitfulness, yet the flimsy sukkah itself, open to the elements, anticipates the vulnerability of winter.

Jewish theology today is afflicted by a gulf between the academic and the congregational—the lived life of "ordinary" Jews. Hoffman constantly opens the doors and windows of Jewish academia to other disciplines—and lets them disturb the pages of a world devoted to the study of classical Jewish text *lishmah*, "for its own sake," and on its own constrained terms. More importantly still, he is a rare liminal figure, living at the edge of both the academic and congregational, constantly facilitating connection and interaction between the two.

When I was a student at Leo Baeck College in the early 1970s, my German Jewish refugee teachers would mention Franz Rosenzweig's *The Star of Redemption* in hushed, reverential terms. Yet I was not able to share their passion until I discovered that Rosenzweig had embarked on a promising academic career as a Hegelian academic but renounced it to become a Jewish educator. He saw that the Jews of his time were in danger of being blown away by the bracing post-Enlightenment winds and assimilating into the supposedly identity-neutral world of modernity, so he left the cloisters to establish his Lehrhaus in Frankfurt. Like Hoffman, he did not limit himself to the world of the academy, despite abundant ability and opportunity. His focus was, as Hoffman might say, "beyond the text."

I was on a Zoom call with Hoffman—technology is strictly neutral and, therefore, open to appalling misuse, but being able to talk like that, study to study with only irritating time zones between us, is a modern miracle. He told me with great excitement that he had just made a discovery and ordered me to take down Tractate *P'sachim* (the section of the Mishnah dealing with the Passover seder) from the shelf and turn to chapter ten. He then embarked on a minute, enthusiastic textual examination, academically rigorous but never, as with some, to the point of rigor mortis!

He explained that the familiar phrase *Mah nishtanah halailah hazeh*, usually translated in English Haggadot as "Why is this night different from all other nights?," had originally neither introduced the familiar Four Questions nor even been a question itself. Rather, it was an exclamation: "How different this evening is from all other evenings!" The seder is an occasion for celebration, discussion, debate, and impromptu questions, suggesting a revival of the influence of the Greek symposium meal—with its emphasis on discussion and debate, though still lubricated by four cups of wine!

This is the second unique aspect of Hoffman's Judaism. Not only does he open the windows of academic Judaism to the invigorating breezes of other disciplines, but also and even more importantly perhaps, he brings the world of academic theology into the lived lives of contemporary Jews—for example, by bringing mastery of text study to bear on easing the arthritic bones of the seder. His ever-developing personal Haggadah is living liturgy, and his innovative ceremony resolving the wasteful nature of the cup of Elijah is an example of his unquenchable creativity. Like

Synagogue 2000, Hoffman's not-for-profit dedicated to both studying and transforming synagogues in the 1990s and 2000s, we have irrefutable proof of his dancing feet in both camps.

When it comes to liturgy, and in particular the siddur, Hoffman's essay challenges us to look with both eyes at the way in which liturgy is received by congregants. Drawing on anthropology, he asks how liturgy, an established academic subject, and the siddur into which so much expertise has been poured are actually used by the individual "pray-er." This is not a detached exercise by an external observer, but rather a committed invitation to those who make use of the liturgy to ask themselves what it is they think they are doing.

Anthropologist Clifford Geertz's question about "what is getting said" has sparked in Hoffman a way of looking at the still-familiar—Jews in shul—and asking an unfamiliar question: Does the praying emerge from a significantly lived Jewish life?

In answering this question, the denomination of the person praying does not matter, nor does the style of prayer, the *minhag*. What matters is whether prayer is bound up with an observable pattern of Jewish living or whether it is largely detached from the rest of the person's daily life. If it's the former, part of a recognizable Jewish life, then how the person praying explains it—meaning their understanding of what they are doing—is secondary. But if the connection has little substance—in the way that the concept of *tikun olam* (repairing the world) can be misused to provide a Jewish-style label for current secular notions of social justice—then Hoffman would want to prompt in the pray-er deeper self-questioning. That prayer book in your hands, he has said, contains the "CliffsNotes" of Judaism; are you prepared to try singing at least some of the lines with conviction, or are you content with a trite melody and banal words, not Judaism but Judaism-lite?

I love Hoffman's metaphor of the siddur as the CliffsNotes of Judaism. In my most recent book, *Being Jewish Today*, I tried to explore my own reactions to synagogue services once I retired from the pulpit and ceased being an orchestrator of prayer and had become an ordinary "Jew in the pew"—only more so, hypercritical as only a rabbi can be![1]

I'm extremely grateful for the rich and extensive study anthologies that Rabbis Lionel Blue and Jonathan Magonet have made the hallmark of British Reform prayer books—CliffsNotes of the highest class.[2] The service became, for me, a backdrop for exploring issues of theology and personal belief prompted by arresting and provocative texts both ancient and modern.

I discovered after some months that the text of the liturgy receded, leaving an internal dialogue that was an angry, challenging, but sometimes genuine conversation. At that point, I was reminded of a familiar dialogue in which a congregant says to the rabbi, "I don't need to come to your synagogue to pray. I can pray anywhere, even in a field if I choose," to which the rabbi responds, "I understand, but I have to say that in all the many years I've been a rabbi, I haven't seen a single person standing in a field praying." Similarly, despite my ambivalence about other rabbis' shuls, I realized that I needed the backdrop of a synagogue service to engage with God in prayer.

I spent the bulk of my career on the front line of Jewish life: in a congregation; developing a Reform Jewish religious, educational, and cultural center; as head of the Movement for Reform Judaism in Britain.[3] Then I moved on to the Leo Baeck College as professor of Jewish theology and thought to write a book of theology—and found that I could explore its core only back in the synagogue.

My discovery exemplifies the truth Hoffman has always pursued: the need to bridge the worlds of academia and the lived life beyond its cloister. Which is why a Zoom call with Hoffman—for instance, to discuss the nature of truth—is as invigorating as the windows he opens through anthropology and the contemporary illumination he sheds through text scholarship. The conversation is always, on his part at least, *l'shem shamayim*, "for the sake of heaven," never in the spirit of self-seeking.[4]

CHAPTER 24

In Conversation with Silence

Emily Langowitz

Emily Langowitz is a rabbi and Jewish engagement and learning manager at the Union for Reform Judaism.

What is Judaism? "Judaism," I have often heard Rabbi Larry Hoffman suggest, "is a conversation." It is a conversation among contemporary Jews, sacred texts, and the Jewish people of the past, present, and future. Beyond our texts and beyond their writers, however, lie the unwritten stories of the Jewish people. For every sacred text that made its way into the canon, for every prayer that found its way into our siddurim (prayer books), there were hundreds of other messages that went undocumented. These unwritten words, now lost to us because of systems of power at work both internal and external to the Jewish community, have as much to teach us as those that were preserved. What is Judaism? It is a spiritual exercise in learning to converse with silence.

The Jewish tradition, as it has been passed down to us, already offers several models for how we might listen to its silences. Two of the Hebrew Bible's most powerful images depict God not in powerful, loud, spacious grandeur, but in stillness and withdrawal. First, when Moses asks to witness God's presence atop Sinai, God denies him, telling him, "You will see My back; but My face must not be seen" (Exodus 33:23).[1] This passage calls us to consider the power of seeking God's face when it is hidden. Generations later, Elijah the Prophet undergoes a parallel experience on the same mountain.[2] The prophet tells us clearly, "The Eternal was not in the wind; . . . the Eternal was not in the earthquake; . . . the Eternal was not in the fire." For Elijah, God is most present not in what he can see and hear and feel, but in what he can't: "the voice of still silence" (I Kings 19:11–12).[3]

The importance, and the sacredness, of that silence comes across in the way Jewish tradition approaches textual interpretation. The project of midrash is an exercise in conversing with silence. When there is something missing in the Torah's text, a key fact or detail, or a question unanswered, midrash steps in to find a way to see beyond what is written. Jewish tradition views this work to uncover the hidden voices within the text's silences not as subversive, not as an inferior, subjective application of the morals and mores of its writers, but rather as equivalent to revelation. One such midrash makes this point by comparing the silence of Elijah's revelation to that of Moses:

> Said Rabbi Abahu . . . in the name of Rabbi Yochanan: . . . When the Holy Blessed One gave the Torah, no bird chirped, no fowl fluttered, no ox lowed, the angels did not fly, the seraphim did not utter the K'dushah [their customary liturgical recitation], the sea did not roar, the creatures did not speak; the universe was silent and mute. And the voice came forth: "I am the Infinite, your God."[4]

How powerful it is, how utterly magnificent, to listen for the revelation that pours forth from the absence of sound!

Contemporary thinkers, particularly modern feminist scholars, help expand our understanding of how we might use the ancient techniques of midrash to bring as-yet-unheard voices to light. Judith Plaskow, in her groundbreaking work *Standing Again at Sinai*, writes, "Midrash is not a violation of historical canons but an enactment of commitment to the fruitfulness and relevance of biblical texts. . . . Remembering and inventing together help recover the hidden half of Torah, reshaping memory to let women speak."[5] I have been inspired by Plaskow and other scholars like her in my own work to fill silences within Jewish tradition. My rabbinical thesis and subsequent teaching and writing focus on expanding the conversation around abortion, reproductive justice, and Jewish values. For much of Jewish history, pregnant people's voices were not considered authoritative on these subjects and were rarely recorded. To converse with such a silence requires listening to those voices in the here and now and drawing on contemporary scholarship to engage in Plaskow's task of "remembering and inventing together."

We might, for example, reimagine the story in the Book of Genesis of Abraham's hospitality to the visiting angels, who announce Sarah's imminent pregnancy (Genesis 18). Pregnancy, according to some feminist theorists, is an act of hospitality, which, to be ethical, cannot be coerced. We might therefore re-envision Sarah's laughter, upon learning that she will give birth at the age of ninety, representing not a distrust of God's plan, as some commentators have it, but a joyful choosing of her own pregnancy—willing hospitality. Such a reinterpretation grants agency to an archetypal woman whose voice has for too long been silenced.

Hoffman has explained that prayer is not simply words on a page but a drama unfolding, a ritual that helps a community articulate its most central values. It is perhaps the clearest example of the Jewish attempt to be in dialogue with the silence and stillness that can carry the utmost holiness, as the Psalmist writes, "To You, silence is praise" (Psalms 65:2). But when the tradition's silence means that voices of those on the outside of power are not heard, when it means Jews cannot see themselves in our sacred texts, when it means that the fullness of God and Torah goes unrevealed, then we are obligated to speak into that silence and to listen for what it commands us in return.

Section 9

Authenticity

This essay also comes from Rabbi Larry Hoffman's 1973 address to the biennial convention of the Union of American Hebrew Congregations (UAHC; later, Union for Reform Judaism) and has been subsequently and substantially reworked over many years. Here, the question Hoffman poses is more general: How can religious people who embrace change claim the mantle of authenticity? It is followed by three reflections on the same question by Hoffman's students.

But what counts as authentic Jewish prayer? The practice of the founding rabbis who had no written siddur altogether? *Minhag Bavel* (Babylonian tradition, that is, the tradition of Iraq in the ninth century) or *Minhag Eretz Yisrael* (tradition from the Land of Israel before the Crusades)? Our first extant siddur (circa 860 CE) was composed by the Gaon, or head of Babylonian Jewry, in Baghdad; Jews in the Land of Israel still had no single siddur. We know from archives of the Cairo Jewish community contained in the genizah (repository of unwanted Hebrew texts) of the Ben Ezra Synagogue that their prayers were often wildly different from the Babylonian ones. Jews worldwide follow the Baghdad prototype, not the Land of Israel alternatives, because the Crusades wiped out the options from the Land of Israel. Nonetheless, in about 920 CE, another Gaon (Saadia) promulgated his own prayer book, an "enlightened" version, with proper grammatical constructions and even philosophical meditations that look suspiciously like alternatives to the Amidah (the thrice-daily obligatory prayer), perhaps because people had philosophical trouble with the traditional wording.

Which of these traditions is "authentic"? Aren't they all authentic to their own time and place?

Problems arise when we ignore history and think our own way of praying is the only authentic one; when, that is, we weaponize our own worship to attack the worship of others. Such attacks are not new; they have been endemic, because our identities are at stake. Were our worship inauthentic, then our identities must be as well. Traditionalist mitnagdim (opponents) attacked "upstart" Chasidim (adherents of the popular spirituality of the Ba'al Shem Tov and his successors in Eastern Europe) in the eighteenth century; a century later, Reform Judaism was targeted by them both. The Reform movement, meanwhile, throughout its early years, attacked those who sought to adhere to long-standing norms as obscurantists or worse. In 1945, after Mordecai Kaplan published a siddur guided by his Reconstructionist philosophy, the Orthodox Agudas HaRabonim excommunicated him.

One more thing: It is worship that delivers our sense of what Jewish tradition is. Hardly anyone has the time to read the whole Bible, let alone the Talmud and rabbinic literature, more broadly. Our worship, therefore, condenses the wisdom of the Jewish past into a delivery system for the average person, whose experience of Judaism comes largely from Jewish worship and ritual. If we see our worship as authentic, we see the tradition it portrays as authentic also. And we proudly own it.

Yes: we own it. The word *tradition* comes from the Latin *tradere*, which means "passing along, from one person to another." The Hebrew agrees: the word for tradition, *masoret*, comes from the Hebrew root *masar*, meaning "to transmit." In English common law, "tradition" meant the passing along of real estate, not just ideas or customs. Tradition *had to be owned or it ceased existing*. Religion is the process of keeping tradition alive by handing it over to new generations who decide to own it, and that "handing over" takes place whenever Jews pray.

CHAPTER 25

Creating Authentic Jewish Prayer

Jill Abramson

Jill Abramson is the director of the Debbie Friedman School of Sacred Music at Hebrew Union College–Jewish Institute of Religion in New York.

Most of us seek experiences that are authentic and genuine; we are skeptical when things feel phony. So, too, with worship: we are drawn to services that we deem to be authentic, while at the same time acknowledging that there can be multiple expressions of authenticity.

Rabbi Larry Hoffman asks, "What counts as authentic Jewish prayer?" As he points out, problems inevitably arise when we think of our own style of prayer as the authentic one. Given the multiplicity of authentic prayer styles, how, then, can we understand what it means to be authentically Jewish?

At its core, authenticity demands knowledge. Have I studied the meaning of a prayer? Do I know the source of a melody? Do I comprehend the theology? When we understand the origins of a prayer and its evolution, we bring authenticity to our worship. While not all of us have the luxury of time to study, each opportunity to learn can expand our understanding. More broadly speaking, an awareness of Jewish culture as it has developed over time can enrich our worship and deepen our spirituality.

As a young cantorial student at Hebrew Union College–Jewish Institute of Religion, I decided that if I were to engage in any kind of creative departure, such as composing new music, I first needed to know what I was departing *from*. I realized I had to study in depth a wide range of musical styles of past generations as well as gain fluency in the newest expressions of musical creativity. The Psalmist implores us to "Sing unto God a new song" (e.g., Psalms 96:1, 98:1), and I wanted to express myself in a contemporary musical idiom with an understanding of, and reverence for, music of past generations. And so I entered Hoffman's and his colleagues' classrooms and immersed myself in the history of Jewish prayer and music.

There are other types of authenticity: Can I lead worship with good conscience? That is, do I feel genuine as I recite the prayers of my ancestors? Do I feel sincere when I adapt their words and innovate? (Note that I am speaking of a feeling here rather than knowing; authenticity is sometimes also a matter of emotion.) Furthermore, is what I am doing the right thing? Do I have confidence in the integrity of my intentions and my actions? Or, if I don't have complete confidence, am I confident that through ongoing experimentation, I will end up doing the right thing? And as I work with other prayer leaders and worshippers, how best can I enable their trust in me? How do I honor other people's trust?

The affect of a leader of prayer conveys authenticity: a non-anxious presence, a balance of confidence and humility, an ability to publicly represent a range of human emotion, from overflowing joy to quiet introspection.

Prayer is simultaneously personal and communal. Leading prayer authentically recognizes both. If the leader of prayer is sincere, they will know themselves, and those who are being guided in prayer will know. Honor your heart and your hearers. They are both listening carefully.

CHAPTER 26

Seeking Templates for Authentic Prayer

Yael Splansky

Yael Splansky is the senior rabbi of Holy Blossom Temple in Toronto.

Rabban Gamliel would proclaim and say, "Any student whose insides are not like their outsides may not enter the study hall." On the day Rabbi Elazar ben Azarya succeeded him, however, the guard at the door was dismissed, and permission was granted for all students to enter.

—Babylonian Talmud, *B'rachot* 28a

Rabban Gamliel protected and preserved the chain of tradition by instituting an "authenticity check" at the door. Rabbi Elazar ben Azarya was equally committed to authenticity, but his policy of inclusion inspired it more than required it. As Rabbi Larry Hoffman writes, "Problems arise when we ignore history and think our own way of praying is the only authentic one; when, that is, we weaponize our own worship to attack the worship of others." For Elazar ben Azarya, the most effective way to strengthen the chain of tradition was to draw people into the conversation, shape their ways of thinking, and influence their choices. Just as in his teaching, Hoffman draws in students of all kinds and reveals for them authentic paths for engaging with old Jewish ideas and new applications.

What is authenticity? The word can mean one of two things. One meaning has to do with traditional origins: an authentic document, authentic Italian dishes. The other has to do with being true to one's own beliefs, spirit, or character. The former requires the consensus of the collective. The latter can only be determined by ourselves, for ourselves. The former resembles *keva*, the fixed components of Jewish prayer. The latter resembles *kavanah*, the intention an individual person brings to the prayer experience. Is the prayer constructed authentically—in theology, melody, choreography, poetry, form, and setting? The collective decides. Is the prayer delivered authentically? Only the individual can know. Without the authentic expression of the individual, the rituals become rote and the prayer only performative. Without the people's seal of authenticity, worship is at risk of being creative art at best or perhaps idolatry at worst.

In a world in which someone is always trying to sell us something, we place a high premium on both aspects of authenticity. The collective judges whether something "smells" authentic, whether it has the flavor of tradition, and whether it will have staying power. In a world growing more cynical by the hour, to pray with sincerity is an act of protest. For an individual to say "I believe" takes courage. Authentic prayer springs from the self, but it is not directed toward the self. It is directed Godward and authenticated by the collective—past, present, and future.

In searching for a template for authentic prayer, Jewish tradition offers us the G'ulah, a prayer for redemption that follows the twice-daily recitation of the Sh'ma. It begins with the word *emet* (truth) and describes the components of "authentic prayer." The version of this prayer said in the morning uses eight pairs of adjectives: "True and immutable, correct and enduring, upright and faithful, beloved and cherished, desired and pleasant, awesome and mighty, affixed and accepted, good and beautiful is this for us and for all eternity." In poetic form, these assertions of faith are authenticated by the collective. They are tried and true and universally recognized by the Jewish people. "Throughout the generations, God endures and God's name endures." It goes on and on like this, driving home the point of an unbroken chain: "God's words are alive and enduring, faithful and desirable, forever and to all eternity, for our ancestors and for us, for our children and for our generations and for all generations of the descendants of Israel, Your servants."[1]

As the G'ulah unfolds, however, the second meaning of "authentic" comes into play. Continuity for its own sake is not enough: "God answers

God's people when they cry out to God." In turn, there came a new song: "With a new song the redeemed praised Your great name at the seashore." The authentic cry is answered, and the answer inspires a new song.

Just as our ancestors' personal experience at the sea gave rise to a collectively sanctioned innovation in prayer, the "new song," so, too, do we, their descendants, reenact the scene each day: to cry out, to be answered, and in turn, to create a new song in our own time. Our people's relationship with the Divine is constant, but its expression must be renewed in each generation. This is how Jewish authenticity evolves. The stories and scripts of our ancestors inspire and model for us how to write our own new song. What is old becomes new again, but not altogether new. With a little luck and a lot of practice, we can discover what is both "true and immutable."

The Babylonian Talmud records two versions of a story about people who challenge the distinction between the tried and true and our own new songs.[2] The story recounts Moses's prayer near the end of his life—"the great, the mighty, and the awesome God" (Deuteronomy 10:17)—as an archetypal prayer and fixes it in the thrice-daily prayer service known as the Amidah (lit. "standing prayer"). It notes, further, that the prophet Jeremiah, who witnessed the destruction of Jerusalem's First Temple, used two out of these three terms of praise, "great" and "mighty," but omitted "awesome" from his personal prayers: "O great and mighty God whose name is Adonai of Hosts" (Jeremiah 32:18). Similarly, the prophet Daniel, who saw his people enslaved in his own time, used only two of these terms of praise, omitting "mighty": "the great and awesome God" (Daniel 9:4). Our sages ask, "How could Jeremiah and Daniel uproot an ordinance instituted by Moses?"

Rabbi Elazar (a different Elazar from Elazar ben Azarya) explains, "They did so because they knew that the Holy One Blessed be God is truthful and hates falsehood." Jeremiah had not personally perceived God's attribute of awesomeness; similarly, Daniel had not personally perceived his might. Therefore, they could offer only prayers that authentically reflected their own life experiences.

Rabbi Elazar praises Jeremiah and Daniel for their commitment to pray only what they mean and mean what they pray. But in the Talmudic discussion, the last word goes to Rabbi Joshua ben Levi, who commends later Jewish leaders of the generations after Jeremiah and Daniel for "return[ing] the crown of the Holy One to its former glory" by establishing the original script, all three fixed attributes of praise, as the central text of the Jewish liturgy. In other words, there seems to be a hierarchy of needs in prayer. We should pray only what is authentic to our experience, but it is better still to find a way to infuse the original words with new meaning, so we can offer them in all sincerity.

The Talmud also relates the story of an unnamed prayer leader who stood before the synagogue ark and expanded on Moses's original prayer, saying: "God, the great, the mighty, and the awesome, the powerful, and the strong, and the fearless."[3] Rabbi Chanina was part of the congregation that day and later scolded the prayer leader for doubling the number of praises for God: "It is comparable to a man who possessed many thousands of golden dinars, yet they were praising him for owning a thousand silver ones." That is, all the praises one can lavish upon the Eternal God are as nothing but a few silver dinars. Reciting a litany of praise does not enhance God's glory, which is priceless. Therefore, we ought to stick to the script we have inherited from Moses. Its provenance makes it, too, priceless.

This story establishes another hierarchy: The original prayer is more preferable than one's sincere and innovative prayer. Rabbi Chanina, as the authoritative voice of the community, delivers a lesson in humility to the nameless prayer, just as the act of prayer is itself a practice in humility.

A simple reading of these two stories might be "Less is more." But, taken together, they demonstrate that authentic prayer is bottomless, but not boundless. We bring infinite *kavanah* to our prayers, and only we can judge our own devotion. Yet the breadth of the *keva*, in contrast, is not infinite. Over all the time and space Jewish prayer has traveled, it has seen expansive, but not boundless, innovations. Considering our migrations and outside influences, we have remarkably managed to retain its core texts and forms. This, too, is an act of faith. This healthy tension between the authenticity of the self and the authenticity of the collective is one of the unarticulated secrets of Jewish life.

CHAPTER 27

Choose Life

Daniel Reiser

Daniel Reiser is the rabbi of Temple Beth Shalom in Hastings-on-Hudson, New York.

In his biennial convention talk of 1973 and his Israeli Reform movement talk of 2021, Rabbi Larry Hoffman traces how the Jewish liturgical tradition has changed through time and place. Those changes make us ask: What makes a Jewish community's self-expression "authentically Jewish"? In our world forever changed by COVID, it a question that remains as relevant as ever.

In the spring of 2022, as the world slowly emerged from the COVID-19 pandemic, masks were coming off and schools opening up, life was getting back to normal, but many synagogues were emptier than ever. It seemed clear that we had reached a moment in Jewish life that called for urgent change. The pandemic had pulled back the curtain and revealed the weaknesses in our particular form of American Judaism, as so many commentators and community leaders have noted: under-engaged congregants, overworked professionals, expensive dues and tuitions, overstretched budgets, a thin feeling of belonging, only a vague sense of purpose.

These problems had been there all along, but we had ignored them for years, either content with the familiarity of the status quo or too busy tending to the day-to-day issues of congregational life to address them. But now that the status quo had fallen away, we were left with a critical choice. We could either make a heroic effort to reboot a broken system or seize the opportunity to build something anew: to reconsider our purpose, realign our priorities, and rebuild the American synagogue from the ground up.

And then one night, in this moment that called for urgent change, I had a vivid dream: A rabbi I knew and cared about was dying (it was unclear who exactly this was, as is so often the case in dreams). In the middle of the night, I boarded a flight with a group of others who loved this rabbi so that we could sit by the rabbi's bedside. It was an emotional and exhausting farewell.

Later in the dream, I realized that the place we had flown to was the Jewish summer camp I had attended as a child. I wandered over to its chapel in the woods and sat down on a bench, waiting for Shabbat services to begin. But instead of the whole camp of nearly six hundred campers and staff members, there were only a dozen or so people. I asked someone why attendance was so sparse, and they informed me that services were now optional. Looking around, I noticed that nobody was wearing white, which was our camp's custom on Shabbat. When I asked, I was told that we no longer wore white. I awoke feeling a sense of great loss—as if the Jewish world that I had known was coming to an end, as if the Jewish world that so many of us have loved was dying.

It isn't just that synagogue attendance is down. Rather, some of our basic assumptions about organized Jewish life have suddenly proved unstable: the ways in which we gather, what a rabbi should know and be able to do, even what it is that our people are looking for in the first place. It seems as if the world that shaped so many of us might be slipping away, leaving us feeling disoriented, confused, and adrift.

Who, exactly, are we after the things that once defined us have died?

It pains me to acknowledge that even some of our core practices, the things we once believed to be the bread and butter of Jewish life, feel like they have largely grown stale. I am not sure that they can easily be reinvigorated with a few modest adjustments. I fear that we may need to reimagine them from the ground up. Two examples that come to mind are the weekly Torah reading and our worship.

Synagogue Torah study has largely grown stale. There are so many interesting books in the Jewish library; why, week after week, do we limit our curiosity only to a certain prescribed slice of our literary tradition? Year after year, we wade through the dimensions of the Tabernacle, instructions for animal sacrifice, and methods for diagnosing *tzara'at* (a biblical skin disease) when we could be reading an essay on chosenness, a biography of

Maimonides, a reflection on the American Jewish experience, a Yiddish short story, or a modern Israeli poem. If we allowed our imaginations to browse more widely through our vast canon, what new and colorful ideas might emerge from our bimahs and enliven our conversations?

Yet at the same time, what might be lost if the Torah were no longer at the center of our Jewish lives? Would we feel that some core element was missing—as if our Judaism were inauthentic, as if we'd traded in religion for culture? Would we feel that some tie had been severed, detaching us from our ancestors and our Jewish family around the world?

Similarly, the way we worship together has grown stale. Prayer should help us give voice to the deepest parts of our humanity, should help us express through poetry, ritual, and song the parts of ourselves that we usually keep just beneath the surface: our joys, pains, fears, and aspirations. Instead, in many of the synagogues that I have observed, our services are often rote recitation, in which the words, melodies, and choreography often serve not as a vehicle for sincerity and conviction, but rather, I fear, as an obstacle to them. Why do we insist upon making our way through so many pages of the prayer book, dutifully reading responsively when we are told to—when, perhaps, we might more effectively grow attuned to our deepest held beliefs by spending a few quiet moments at home next to the Shabbat candles, silently gazing at the flickering flames? Yet here, too, I have to ask: What might be lost if we decided to close our prayer books more often? Would our Shabbat ritual suddenly feel flimsy, an exercise in self-help, rather than an expression of faith? If we cease chanting Aleinu (a text about the Jewish people's chosenness that concludes worship) or V'ahavta (paragraphs from Deuteronomy enumerating the commandments), might the Sh'ma be the next thing to disappear?

These kinds of questions might make us uneasy—but the realities the pandemic exposed force us to grapple with them. If we push ourselves not just to tinker in the margins, but rather to reconsider even these core elements of synagogue life, imagine the other constructive changes that might flow outward: greater depth, more collaboration, new ways of measuring success, a clearer sense of who we are and what we stand for. This would allow us to transform not only our Jewish institutions but, more importantly, the lives of the people whom those institutions serve.

I recently told a friend (who is also a rabbi) about my dream of the dying rabbi. He reminded me of the scene in the Talmud in which Moses (as if he were in a dream) is transported hundreds of years into the future, to visit the study hall of the great sage Rabbi Akiva—and discovers there a Jewish world that is completely unrecognizable to him.[1] Though the story was familiar to me, I realized for the first time, in light of my dream, that although Moses feels disoriented and confused by the changes he witnesses, he nevertheless realizes something important: that these revolutionary changes represent not the death of Judaism but rather a way for it to continue to live. In the aftermath of the pandemic, we have the opportunity to cultivate an ethos of radical open-mindedness to change, such that we and our descendants fashion new expressions of Jewish life—expressions that were we given the opportunity to observe them generations hence, we would find them as perplexing and amazing as Moses found Akiva's classroom.

Section 10

Healing and Hearing

In 1989, Rabbi Larry Hoffman's teenage daughter was diagnosed with intractable epilepsy. In the years thereafter, Hoffman has been one of the guiding spirits of the Jewish healing movement, an attempt to bring the experience of illness, healing, and mortality to the forefront of Jewish life. What follows is a reflection on the reality of chronic illness and the cultural critic Susan Sontag's trenchant claim that when we are born, we are issued two passports, one to the "kingdom of the well" and the other to the "kingdom of the sick."[1] It is followed by two essays considering other ways in which Jewish wisdom might be deployed to serve those residing in the "kingdom of the sick."

Sociologist Max Weber (1864–1920) thought the highest good was meaningfulness. Happiness may indeed escape us—as it had Weber himself, who battled depression his whole life—but life can at least have meaning, he thought.

Meaning is the way we fit everything together. When something defies connectedness to anything else, we label it meaningless. If it is an actual object, we say it is useless and throw it away. If it is a state of mind or of being, we say it makes no sense, and unable so easily to throw it away, we try valiantly to assign some sense to it. People who suffer want to know that their pain has the kind of moral meaning that responds to the transcendent question: "Why?"

That is where religion comes in, for religion supplies transcendent meanings. If religion cannot end suffering, it should at least make suffering sufferable. Sufferers are sinners, perhaps, or the objects of God's inscrutable will. So say the experts from the kingdom of the well; residents of the kingdom of the sick have their doubts. And so they should. The search for meaning may be ubiquitous; meaning's existence may not. Sickness may have no meaning at all.

The essayist Annie Dillard pictures schizophrenics as finding meaning in random patterns of raindrops and a psychologist as finding meanings in the schizophrenics' "meanings"; we assume the schizophrenics' meanings are senseless, while the researcher's meanings are not.[2] Are our theological meanings about illness more like schizophrenics' meanings about raindrops or more like researcher's meanings about schizophrenics? Some things (random raindrops) may have no transcendent religious meaning.

By analogy, Susan Sontag thinks art is not necessarily about anything; it just is. Art critics should show that it is what it is, rather than what it means. Art interpretation, she complains, tames what it interprets.[3] When it comes to illness, theologians are like art critics, charged with showing that suffering is what it is, not taming it by assigning it moral meaning.

The philosopher Ludwig Wittgenstein correctly remarks, "Certain things cannot be put into words. . . [they] make themselves manifest. They are what is."[4] Surely suffering is among them. Some religious people say illness is divine punishment, a proposition Wittgenstein would deny—even though there is no evidence one way or the other. He simply thinks differently. "I say different things to myself," he concludes. "I have different pictures."[5] What are pictures if not a way of showing?

What, then, is prayer, not in the kingdom of the well, where suffering is hypothetical, but in the kingdom of the sick, where it is all too real? It is best described as "on the spot" photography of the ultimate human challenge: a human condition that makes no sense. Its very power lies in the fact that posing no question, it pretends to no answer. The most ardent skeptic should dispense with argumentation and just look at the picture.

Prayer is not description (despite its descriptive language), nor is it petition (despite its patent requests). No scientific reality need correspond to the descriptions we give, and no supernatural power need respond to the requests we make. Liturgy lets us show what ordinary conversation precludes; it is the last and best outlet for those who suffer, and it is also the best way for the rest of us to find the empathy needed to make their suffering sufferable.

CHAPTER 28

Making Suffering Sufferable

Nicole Roberts

Nicole Roberts is senior rabbi of North Shore Temple Emanuel in Sydney, Australia.

Last week, I sat in the ophthalmologist's office as she studied the concerning results of my visual field test. When she paused in reciting a litany of conditions that might be causing the impairment, I contributed, nervously, "Could it be from eye strain? I spend a lot of time at the computer. Could it be high blood sugar? I eat too many sweets. Should I be wearing better sunglasses?" Her response, while not a diagnosis, brought a wave of relief, which endures even as I await further test results: "It's not from anything you've done." *It's not from anything I've done!* Just plain old bad luck. Arbitrary, really. How strangely comforting to hear this.

I had felt a similar sense of relief once before. The last person to reassure me that a misfortune was "not from anything you've done" was not a vision expert but rather a professor in rabbinical school, after one particularly difficult experience resulted in heartbreak, a fierce sense of injustice, and despair. I felt held by words of encouragement from so many wise rabbis around me, but the most soothing balm for my soul was when my Bible professor, sensing my agitation, called me in for a conversation about the Book of *Kohelet* (Ecclesiastes).

I do not recall which passage he recited to me. Maybe it was verse 9:11: "The race is not won by the swift . . . nor favor by the learned, for the time of mischance comes to all." Or perhaps it was verse 8:14: "There are righteous visited with that befitting the wicked." These and a host of other verses in the text speak to my professor's confidence—and *Kohelet*'s—that I did not *do* anything wrong to cause my misfortune. I still hear my professor's voice, proclaiming, "It's *arbitrary!*" This release from the thought that my pain bore *meaning* was a gift, which did not end my suffering but did, in Rabbi Larry Hoffman's words, "make suffering sufferable."

During that difficult period in seminary, I also found relief in the Book of Psalms. I could never personally relate to the psalms until, in that time of anguish, I was asked to read one aloud in class. The verses contained words of angry protest, longing, and helplessness—raw expressions of fear and frustration—which spoke to me so profoundly that I almost burst into tears. I read the psalm and felt instantly that my tormented soul had company. Generally, psalms express emotions more dramatic than those that I feel day-to-day. But few words resonate as deeply as a psalm on those occasional days when I have really been through the wringer.

Such psalms, along with those verses from *Kohelet*, are the sort of "'on the spot' photography" that Hoffman describes. These texts depict "the ultimate human challenge: a human condition that makes no sense" and "pretends to no answer." Why do bad things happen to good people? It's arbitrary, it's happened for millennia, and someone in our tradition wasn't afraid to be brutally honest about how it feels. These particular writings are among Judaism's greatest gifts to those who suffer, in every era.

Prayer may also be such a gift. Hoffman seems to think so, and I want to believe him. This, however, has not been my experience of prayer.

Let me qualify that statement. Private prayer works for me when I am going through a difficult time. By "works," I do not mean that my prayers change reality, only that they change my frame of mind, enough so that I can get to sleep at night. At the end of a hard day, when my mind races to find solutions to impossible problems and worries, often relief *only* comes with private prayer. I outline the problems and admit to God (and myself) that I have no idea how to solve them. I ask for help, laying my trust in God to guide my next steps. I may have been lying awake for hours, but once I finally begin to pray, I often doze off before I ever get to "amen." Articulating my worries, disappointments, and disillusionments with sincerity, and not bearing them on my shoulders alone, brings relief.

Such relief does not come, however, when I pray in community. I enjoy many aspects of communal prayer: solidarity, voices merged in song, recitation of cherished texts, and *ru'ach* (collective energy). But while

Hoffman writes that liturgy is the "best outlet for those who suffer," I do not see suffering depicted in our liturgy. Why? Because my community, like most Reform communities, prays together only on Shabbat, and Shabbat liturgy does not countenance much suffering. Suffering is just not what Shabbat is about. On Shabbat, we are meant to be grateful for what we have and to express that gratitude. The psalms of praise and gratitude that we sing on Shabbat are not the ones that speak the brutal, honest truth about how hard life can be. We cannot pray the petitionary prayers of the weekday Amidah (thrice-daily liturgy), asking God for help. On Shabbat, our "foretaste of the world to come," we are to envision ourselves as "dreamers upon return to the Promised Land," not as down-trodden exiles crying "by the rivers of Babylon" (even though the latter may better reflect how we actually feel).[1] Might a fuller communal prayer life that extends beyond Shabbat prayers be our passport between these two worlds?

Without any experience of weekday communal prayer, we live only one-seventh of what a Jewish prayer life is meant to feel like. In most of our congregations, communal prayer exists in just two dimensions: coming or not coming on Shabbat, and most choose not to come. How many who have vacated our now sparsely filled sanctuaries found our Shabbat-only liturgy an insufficient salve for their aching souls or, worse, irrelevant in their time of pain? ("Why should I offer praise and thanks to God when I feel like this?") Shabbat liturgy does not always meet us where we are. On Shabbat, anything but contentment with our portion is off the table.

In seminary, we learn other prayer postures, literally. Like the Tacha-nun (supplication) prayer recited after the weekday Amidah, seated and bent over as if we are unable to bear the weight of our own head, a posi-tion that depicts how we actually feel when we are in anguish and resort to prayer. We learn that there is a different psalm recited each day of the week, including some that blatantly question why the wicked prosper while the righteous live in a state of anxiety. We learn petitionary prayers—thirteen of them!—that are all replaced on Shabbat by a single one, the "sanctification of the day." But just because rabbis study these aspects of a fuller prayer life does not mean that our congregations experience them by osmosis. What if our congregants encountered communal prayer that depicted a fuller range of emotions?

What if we taught to our communities that none other than King David cried out in despair, "I am weary with groaning. Every night I drench my bed . . . in tears?" (Psalm 6:7). Tachanun begins with this depiction—these anguished words, said while resting our head on our arm. Surrounded by others who have assumed the same posture, a sufferer among us might feel less alone, even soothed.

Tachanun does not ascribe meaning to human distress; instead, as when I pray alone in the dark of night, it expresses, "We do not know what to do . . . for we have been brought very low" (II Chronicles 20:12). We do not have answers. We are at a loss. And so we "let go and let God." That is, we let God bear the weight of our heavy thoughts and guide our way forward, as we read in the final section of Tachanun: "Our eyes are turned to You . . . we place our hope in you" (II Chronicles 20:12). Maybe God can help.

Perhaps the era of online services will make weekday prayer possible in Reform congregations—adding, ironically, a third dimension to our communal prayer life: a liturgy that meets us where we are on those days when we feel less than content with our portion. On Shabbat, when giving thanks after a meal, we recite, "Those who sow in tears shall reap in joy" (Psalm 126:5). Maybe there would be more room in our hearts for praise and gratitude on Shabbat if, during the week, we poured out our hearts to God. Maybe we could lift our voices higher on Shabbat if, during the week, we laid down our heads in prayer, letting God help and heal us.

CHAPTER 29

The Time Zone of the Kingdom of the Sick

Elliot Kukla

Elliot Kukla is a rabbi, author, visual artist, and activist in Oakland, California.

It's my job to be with people on the worst day of their lives. I have spent the past fifteen years offering spiritual care to the dying, sick, and bereaved. I am the rabbi you call when the phone rings with the results of a bad CAT scan and suddenly everything you have carefully built comes tumbling down. As Susan Sontag famously noted, each of us has a passport to two countries: "the kingdom of the well" and "the kingdom of the sick." Sooner or later, we all use that second passport.[1]

In the face of suffering, it is tempting to try to fix the unfixable. Rabbi Larry Hoffman encourages us to consider how to speak meaningfully to people for whom words often seem hollow. When my sick clients first tell me their stories, I usually find myself saying some version of "I'm so sorry, that really sucks." They often respond with surprise. After all, I'm a rabbi there to offer spiritual comfort; aren't I going to try to convince them that "everything happens for a reason" or that God will heal them? However, I have learned that cheering advice only serves to abandon my clients who find themselves in the already isolating geography of disease.

Illness is more than a professional interest for me. I am also chronically ill and intimately familiar with the kingdom of the sick and the pitfalls of trying to rationalize its mysterious terrain. Just a few days after my wedding in 2013, I woke up with the worst headache of my life and never got better. Eventually, after months of seeking answers, I was diagnosed with a neurological manifestation of the autoimmune disease lupus.

For nearly five years, I drifted in and out of feverish dreams, too heavy with fatigue to feed or bathe myself. My brain was thick with inflammation, and often I would open my mouth and discover I had forgotten my wife's name or find myself lost on the journey from my bathroom to the bedroom. At that time, well-meaning words of advice or encouragement served to distance me further from others. I didn't need explanations or even hope, but companionship and friendship in my bewildering, new life. As Hoffman writes, "When it comes to illness, theologians are like art critics, charged with showing that suffering is what it is, not taming it by assigning it moral meaning."

In those years in bed, I drew on my memory of my clients who welcomed me into their illnesses and on the teachings of disability justice activists. The lives of other sick and disabled people taught me that illness can't be tamed; it's holy in its wildness. The word "holy" in Hebrew, *kadosh*, literally means "set apart." Illness is set apart from the hectic everyday grind. This doesn't mean that being sick is uncommon. In fact, unless you die very young in an accident, virtually everyone will experience illness. And yet, illness remains set apart from the hustle and bustle of everyday social life and our mainstream ideas of "normalcy." So, too, many of the things the Torah refers to as *kadosh* are extremely common. Shabbat, the day of holy rest, happens every week, and each corner of every field is to be left fallow, for those who are hungry, as an act of holiness. These things are common and yet set apart from the everyday—a break from the mundane.

In Judaism, encountering the Divine often provokes *yirah*, which means both "terrible" and "awe-inspiring." My experiences with illness have been exactly both those things. Being sick is terrible in its physical discomfort, stigma, and isolation. And yet illness disturbs our souls and breaks open our hearts, and it can connect us to the suffering of others, to God, and to the deepest parts of the self, thereby evoking awe.

Hoffman suggests that prayer makes "suffering sufferable." Jewish prayer is not rational; we don't expect our prayers for healing to be answered with literal cure. Instead, prayer is a vivid metaphoric language for the inexplicable that allows us to give voice to the spiritual experience of suffering without taming it.

Jewish sacred texts collapse time—past, present, and future. Reciting the daily liturgy, Jews relive the Exodus twice every day, and each silent prayer ends with an invocation of a peaceful time to come. Likewise, when we are sick, we enter a new time zone. The literature and gender studies scholar Ellen Samuels argues that sick people experience reality in "crip time."[2] The term "crip" is used in disability studies as both a reclaimed identity and as a disabled lens for viewing the world. Samuels writes:

> Crip time is time travel. . . . Some of us contend with the impairments of old age while still young; some of us are treated like children no matter how old we get. The medical language of illness tries to reimpose the linear, speaking in terms of the chronic, the progressive, and the terminal, of relapses and stages. But we who occupy the bodies of crip time know that we are never linear, and we rage silently—or not so silently—at the calm straightforwardness of those who live in the sheltered space of normative time.[3]

The time zone of the kingdom of the sick is not just looser. When I got sick, I grieved the loss of normative time. I could no longer count on my body to be able to get out of bed each day, and I mourned being able to imagine my life as a linear progression of stages and achievements. I also lamented the loss of being able to be casual about things like meals running late or missing a nap. However, it was also liberating to let go of the heaviness of constantly holding onto hope for an imagined future and begin to live in the more emergent and mindful present.

So what can the healthy offer when visiting loved ones and community members dwelling in the kingdom of the sick? Perhaps most importantly, the simple knowledge that all that divides us is timing. Eventually, everyone will get to know that kingdom and come to let go of the neat progression of linear time. When it is our turn to arrive in the place of sickness, we find ourselves not just in a new geography, but in a new time zone. What is needed from visitors is not well-meaning advice, but travel companions who can traverse space and time to make sure that we are not alone.

Section 11

I Do Believe

In 1996, concern about a perceived endemic lack of belief among American Jews led Commentary *magazine to invite several Jewish scholars and leaders to opine about "the state of Jewish belief." Could North American Jews undergo a "revival"?* Commentary *asked. The essay below is adapted from Rabbi Larry Hoffman's reply, and it is followed by two reflections on what Jewish belief might entail today.*

We suffer less from lack of belief than from inadequate language to express it. How can we believe what we do not even know how to say? Conversations about belief should not make honest people feel guilty for doubting what they think everyone else knows for sure. We can confirm or deny belief in "God," "revelation," and so forth only by asking first what these might mean rephrased for modern ears.

Take the Sh'ma and Its Blessings, the daily liturgical staple that affirms our faith in one sole God. Most people think the Sh'ma is a simple one-liner that asserts our faith that "God is One." Actually, it is the centerpiece for three related prayers surrounding it—prayers that affirm, as well, our faith that this one sole God (a) creates all things, (b) reveals Torah to Israel, and (c) promises redemption. Hence the standard holy triad of our *de facto* liturgical creed: Creation, Revelation, and Redemption.

But these titles—Creation, Revelation, and Redemption—are not as old as we think. They are just English equivalents of the nomenclature invented by nineteenth-century German theologians as their own way of understanding the ancient Hebrew. They became canonized, as it were, by the philosopher Franz Rosenzweig in his 1921 masterpiece *The Star of Redemption*. But, however much theologians may admire them, these three terms have lost all religious meaning for twenty-first-century Jews, for whom "creation" evokes a scientific big bang; "revelation" means a great idea that dawns on us; and "redemption" connotes trading in a reward certificate for the real thing or a baseball pitcher who has lost three straight but redeems himself with a win the game after.

The problem lies in the language, however, not the core ideas themselves. What contemporary concepts capture best this threefold insistence on creation, revelation, and redemption?

My reconception combines time, space, and history. What astounds about the universe is the aesthetic and scientific miracle by which the finely tuned network of natural law accords so beautifully with mathematics. I understand the doctrine of creation as the affirmation that the universe is patterned. Revelation describes my faith that this cosmic order comes with human purpose. The universe is ordered in such a way that we matter in it. As for redemption, purpose within pattern gives us the right to hope; the promise of redemption is the saving grace of hope. Pattern, purpose, and hope are the contemporary equivalents of creation, revelation, and redemption. They sustain us on the tiny bridge of time called history.

Can we still hold onto hope, however, given the horrors of the twentieth century, especially (for Jews) the Holocaust? We can if we recognize history itself as just a bridge in time.

If the age of the universe were a line in space equal to the distance from New York to Los Angeles, Jewish history since Abraham and Sarah would cover only ten feet, and human existence, prehistory and all, would encompass only part of a single span of the Golden Gate or the George Washington Bridge. The Holocaust, therefore, in all its unspeakable horror, is insufficient to shatter optimism. It is, as it were, a blip—albeit a traumatic and tragic one—on the screen of cosmic time. The State of Israel is a similar, albeit positive, tiny step in time, an outpost of hope we must defend, but hardly a sudden sign of imminent messianic victory, as some extremists imagine. Life is lived in the narrowness of bridge spans. Faith is the insistence that the bridge goes somewhere, connecting past and future in a present that has meaning.

CHAPTER 30

Faith and Hope in a Time of Challenge

David H. Ellenson

David H. Ellenson is a rabbi and chancellor emeritus of Hebrew Union College–Jewish Institute of Religion.

From the first moment I studied with Rabbi Larry Hoffman as a student in the New York school of the Hebrew Union College–Jewish Institute of Religion in the fall of 1973, I have been indebted to him not only for the knowledge he has imparted, but also for the unparalleled genius he has always displayed in bringing together and synthesizing Jewish texts and overarching theoretical constructs and frameworks in intellectually provocative and spiritually moving ways.

As I read his *Commentary* selection, I noted that Hoffman structures and lays out his response in clear and logical fashion, moving initially from the problem of how modern people might understand issues of belief in the classical Jewish theological categories of creation, revelation, and redemption to how these issues are addressed in traditional Jewish liturgy. Hoffman notes that the *Sh'ma* and the prayers that surround it express "the standard holy triad of our *de facto* liturgical creed: Creation, Revelation, and Redemption." He continues by pointing out that it was the German Jewish philosopher Franz Rosenzweig who "canonized" these themes in Jewish religious thought in his 1921 *The Star of Redemption*. Here we see Hoffman at his Jewish pedagogical best—embedding his concerns and teachings in the fertile and secure soil of Jewish tradition, while formulating them in conceptually novel ways for his contemporary audience. In so doing, Hoffman anchors us in a rich Jewish narrative while at the same time allowing our current concerns and questions about faith to be part of an ongoing Jewish conversation.

Hoffman asserts that "however much" we may admire Rosenzweig and the teachings and beliefs of our ancestors regarding "creation, revelation, and redemption," we as modern Jews are invited to raise our own voices and build upon the wisdom and tradition of those who came before us. By doing so, he empowers us to recognize that we have the right and, indeed, the obligation to add our certainties and doubts to what is an unending Jewish discussion.

Hoffman himself models this obligation to add to the ongoing discussion by unapologetically proclaiming that these three terms of "creation, revelation, and redemption" have, in fact, "lost all religious meaning for twenty-first-century Jews." His own teaching asserts the right to reconstruct the beliefs of the past to formulate meaningful constructs more resonant with the faith and sensibility of a present-day Jewish community.

I concur with much of the substance of what Hoffman has said. He inspires me to comment on his position and reconceptualize another well-known text of our people: the Book of Genesis and the story told of Creation in its first chapter. In so doing, I entrench my own response to issues of faith in the texts of Jewish tradition, as Hoffman has modeled.

This text begins, "When God [Elohim] was about to create heaven and earth, the earth was a chaos, unformed [*tohu vavohu*], and on the chaotic waters' face there was darkness. Then God's spirit glided over the face of the waters, and God said, 'Let there be light!'—and there was light" (Genesis 1:1–3).[1] Here, in these initial verses, the Torah speaks of "pattern." The universe, the Bible asserts, is at first surely "chaotic, unformed—*tohu vavohu*." God then speaks and creates an ordered natural world, beginning with "Let there be light, and there was light."

This understanding is supported Jewishly by a classical *gematria* (the mode of interpretation based on the numerical equivalency of each Hebrew letter), in which the word for the Divine (*Elohim*) has the numerical value of eighty-six, the same as that of the word for nature, *hateva*. God and nature are intertwined, and in the primordial act of calling the universe into existence, God shapes an amorphous bedlam by imposing form and structure, a pattern, upon the world.

Furthermore, this tale of Creation climaxes on the sixth day, when God, speaking, as traditional Jewish commentary has it, to a divine entourage, states, "Let us make human beings in our image, after our likeness" (Genesis 1:26). Humanity is created in the image of God. As I read this, I understand it to mean that persons are called upon to act as God does. Taken in the context of this entire narrative, the principle of *imitatio Dei* (the imperative for human beings to act like God) means that just as God imposes order and purpose upon the world, so we as humans are asked to do the same. Where there is chaos, we should introduce structure. Where there is darkness, we should strive to provide light. God invites us to be partners with the Divine in the work of this world and to affirm that pattern and purpose can be discovered in the life we forge. We are not born into the world as if by fate. Rather, we are called upon to foster community and meaning through our actions.

It is in the third component of Hoffman's triad, his call for us not to surrender "hope," where I somewhat falter. Of course, Judaism unquestionably teaches that we cannot surrender what Hoffman refers to as "the saving grace of hope." Even events as momentous as the Holocaust and the creation of the State of Israel are, as Hoffman observes, little more than blips in time. Yet, to cite another statement that Franz Rosenzweig once addressed to his mentor the philosopher Hermann Cohen, "*Zeit ists*—it is time," our time and our century, and we cannot so easily ignore the momentous events that have shaped it.[2] And while I try to hold on to the hope that, as Martin Luther King Jr. said, "the arc of the moral universe is long, but it bends towards justice,"[3] my own reading of this moment and the events of our day sadly cause me, more often than I care to admit, to despair. I cannot assert with perfect faith a confidence that the "tiny bridge" of history Hoffman describes will lead to a future replete with "meaning." There is too much evil and imperfection in the world.

I am not happy as I write these last words, and I thank Hoffman for provoking me to think about the deepest sense of reality—faith—that informs the innermost recesses of my being. I have no doubt that I aspire to his faith. I also know that the state of cautious pessimism that characterizes my own fear that the arc of history will not necessarily bend toward justice or repair does not hinder my own efforts to make it otherwise. After all, even if goodness as a motivating source has proved insufficient to ensure the future, human beings are not automatons. Human beings possess the ability to choose, and we can elect not to act in ways that will bring catastrophe upon our nation, our people, and our planet. It may well be that fear of the horror of what could be, not hope of what might be realized, will move humanity to act so that the evil that all too often dominates our world will yet be avoided. This hermeneutic of fear is surely not the last word about our faith. However, it may yet prove to be an appropriate first word out of which "the saving grace of hope" may be affirmed.

CHAPTER 31

Hoffman's Metafaith

Gordon Tucker

Gordon Tucker is a rabbi and vice chancellor for religious life and engagement at the Jewish Theological Seminary and a senior fellow at the Shalom Hartman Institute of North America.

The exceedingly wide community of students and colleagues who have studied with Rabbi Larry Hoffman knows him to be the very epitome of the polymath. Hoffman's wide-ranging scholarship and teaching reflect Samuel David Luzzatto's assertion that nothing Jewish is alien to him, as indeed nothing human has been alien to him.[1] At the center of his vast learning, of course, is the field of liturgy, and that testifies to the deep respect in which Hoffman holds the awesome power of words, words that, as Hoffman has taught us, secrete multiple levels of meaning, all of which call for close attention.

Reflecting on the apparent absence of faith in our contemporary times, Hoffman asserts that this stems from an inadequacy of language. In his illustration, the words "creation," "revelation," and "redemption" classically pointed to what were the three long-standing fundamentals of monotheistic faith: that God created the universe as an act of will, made the divine will known to us through commands, and promised an ultimate salvation from suffering and death to those who prove themselves worthy. Yet these words no longer carry the same meanings for today's Jews, Hoffman writes.

What has happened to create this disconnect and thus to lead to the fallacious conclusion that faith itself—and not simply the words used to speak of faith—has failed? In a word, experience. Life experience is what gave the biblical Job the courage to challenge the conventional verities of faith proffered by his friends, and humanity's accumulation of wisdom in modern times has done the same to traditional formulations of faith—whether through scientific knowledge, or the successes of human reasoning, or catastrophic sufferings from which salvation never came.

Should we then conclude that contemporary culture and a life of faith are simply a bad match? Hoffman is clear about this: "Conversations about belief should not make honest people feel guilty for doubting what they think everyone else knows for sure." That is, their experiences must lead them to a faith that reflects those experiences. Job's ordeals may have led him to reject the faith of his friend Eliphaz, but the fact that he "died old and contented" (Job 42:17) tells us that he achieved a different and better faith. What words might Job have used to describe the faith of his latter days? That there is meaning in being able to forgive—such as forgiving his friends' verbal assaults on him in the midst of his misery—and in discovering transcendent significances—and satisfactions—in building a future through children, even as tragedies of the past never fully heal.

The anthropologist Clifford Geertz paraphrased Max Weber's insight about human culture thus: "Man is an animal suspended in webs of significance he himself has spun."[2] Viewed this way, the need and desire for faith may not change very much, but how we receive and interpret what life brings us creates new stories of faith that require new expression. This is just what is asserted in Hoffman's essay. And consider this: the Geertz/Weber image of a spun web suggests that what is most significant in our lives is our effort to fashion a narrative linking together and making sense of our experiences. I want to suggest that something like this image accounts for Hoffman's invoking the metaphor of a "bridge" in this essay, calling history a bridge that "goes somewhere, connecting past and future in a present that has meaning."

Legal scholar Robert Cover (another polymath) was also fascinated by what bridges represent. Discussing the role of law in society, he wrote that law is—like a spun web—"a bridge in normative space connecting . . . the 'world-that-is' . . . with our projections of alternative 'worlds-that-might-be,'" joining the unredeemed reality inherited from the past to an imagined more perfect future. It takes faith to imagine such a bridge, and, he noted, in a way that echoes Weber, that "each community builds its bridges with the materials of sacred narrative."[3] We can now say, reading Hoffman's reflection on faith, that what Cover asserted about law (halachah, in rabbinic tradition) is true in at least the same measure about narrative itself (aggadah). That is, narrative should be seen as a bridge linking experienced reality to an imagined alternative. In Cover's words, "The commitments that are the material of our bridges to the future are learned and expressed through sacred stories."[4]

What I believe Hoffman is teaching us, through his highly accessible liturgical example of the Sh'ma and the figure of the bridge, is that we have the capacity to reformulate our stories so as to reflect our experiences with honesty, and thereby transform both faith and ourselves. The legal scholar Ron Garet, writing about Cover's work, powerfully summed up its import for human societies with words that we can associate with Hoffman as well: "Given the importance we assign to stories, the role they have always played in our efforts to understand ourselves, we can say with some assurance that . . . the very intuition of self-transformation as a human possibility is a residue of storytelling."[5]

This is the "metafaith" (if I may coin such a term) that Hoffman offers us in this tidy teaching. He offers us faith in the very possibility of holding onto a faith transformed. If we recall that the word "liturgy" stems from ancient roots that together mean "work [service] on behalf of the public," then it is not at all surprising that for a liturgist like Hoffman, who has served the Jewish people prodigiously through writing and teaching, his metafaith turns on our perspicacious use of words.

The Recovery of Hope

The following is an excerpt from a 1996 essay written by Rabbi Larry Hoffman on the occasion of Rabbi Alexander Schindler's retirement as president of the Union of American Hebrew Congregations. The essay sought to counter unease among Reform Jews in the years following the persecution of Russian Jewry, concern with the settlement policies of the State of Israel, the rise of evangelical fundamentalism, and the demographic decline of liberal religious denominations. Hoffman advocates for an ideologically grounded Reform Judaism that speaks to the challenges of the age. The two essays that follow consider how Reform Judaism, and liberal religion generally, might respond to these immense challenges.

Ideas matter. The Rabbis knew that, and so, too, did the founders of Reform Judaism, who did not lack for ideas. The synagogue was the place you went to discover the ideas that make life matter.

Not so today. Synagogues no longer impart ideas; they peddle programs—synagogue conventions feature workshops, not debates. An illustrative case is a temple that attracts members because "the rabbi uses puppets for the kids." What was once enlightenment has become entertainment for children who are scheduled for puppetry between piano and soccer.

Cable television has spawned the verb "channel-surfing," meaning the practice of passing time by clicking the control on the remote control up and down the airwaves to provide diversion with snippets of one program after another. So it goes for human programming too. As long as programs are what synagogues offer, they become part of the diversion industry, fighting for a spot on the dial of real-life pauses that people make as they surf through a busy day.

When synagogue life becomes "programming," people complain of "being programmed." If synagogues do not once again become brokers in ideas, people will turn them off like television sets.

The idea that has mattered most over the last two centuries has been the promise of progress and, with it, the anticipation of better times, what Judaism once called a "Messianic Age," to be realized as part of Israel's mission: Jews allying with non-Jews in pursuit of universal justice, discovering traces of God's holiness along the way. Progress, modernity, autonomy, conscience, holiness, hope itself (for the individual and for history)—these are the very essence of Reform Judaism as we have inherited it. They are under attack, and we need to rescue them as ideas that still matter.

Without Jewish ideas, people do not cease being Jews, but they become Jewish drifters, passing ghost-like through their Jewish lives but lacking in Jewish passion. The professional guardians of Jewish continuity understandably stir things up with whatever works: combating antisemitism; nostalgic memories, maybe; pride in Israel, certainly. When thinking fails, keep busy: raise money; go on marches; program, program, program.

But the mind, like nature, abhors a vacuum. Where old ideas fail, new ones rush in like intellectual breath inhaled by oxygen-starved brain cells coming up for air. Just as near-drowned swimmers breathe whatever they can get, atrophied minds suck up ideas and make of them what they can—for better or for worse. It matters, therefore, what ideas we allow to matter.

If we want continuity, we will have to call into question disillusionment and despair. It is not too late to reaffirm the existence of selves that can make a difference, to raise up unashamedly the banner of prophetic religion, and to rediscover the sacred venture known as life. Reform Jews can resurrect the dead idea of reasonable hope.

The new Reform emphasis on ritual these days has nothing to do with a return to Orthodoxy, but a great deal to do with the human search for ideas.

Ritual should be viewed as an important way for human beings to get at ideas that matter. Picture a gift that you have bought being packaged with wrapping paper ... By analogy, imagine ideas getting wrapped by ritual.

The power of ideas is equivalent to the degree to which they are compelling. But part of the way they compel us is their packaging. Packaging is the way ideas are conveyed to us, and ritual is a powerful conveyor—like great music or an unarguable set of equations. All three have an aesthetic quality; a mathematical proof, for instance, is said to be elegant. Ritual is not just self-satisfying fluff: smells and bells and holding hands and eyes glazed over and closed-off minds. When ritual is done really well, it reveals a new kind of truth; it is a multisensory package that shapes ideas even as it delivers them, providing emotion, intellect, and artistry that combine to compel belief.

Ideas that are ritually construed empower us to do what we would otherwise never have the courage for. Classical Reformers are right to recollect the days when Reform liturgy bespoke dignity of purpose, when rabbis railed against injustice, and when every Jew knew that history is a sacred tale, our lives the latest chapter, inviting us to act as if all good things are possible, as if the Messianic Age is just around the corner, as if perfecting the world itself lies softly in our hands.

CHAPTER 32

Ideas Matter (So Do Symbols)

Gordon W. Lathrop

Gordon W. Lathrop is emeritus professor of liturgy at the United Lutheran Seminary and a pastor in the Evangelical Lutheran Church in America.

Ideas do, indeed, matter.

That is, *good* ideas, ideas that invite communities into the search for justice, into reasonable hope, into following the traces of holiness—these ideas matter immensely. And these ideas can be especially powerful when they come clothed in ritual.

I might say it this way: symbols matter. Then, as the philosopher Paul Ricoeur has said, "the symbol gives rise to thought."[1] Further, symbols are often most available to us when they come woven together in that network of communally enacted symbols we call ritual.

But there are problems. For one thing, the presence of despair and the absence of reliable communal meanings are even more characteristic of our current times than they were of the 1990s in which Rabbi Larry Hoffman wrote this essay. And the symbols and rituals we use are, unfortunately, not necessarily up to the task of giving rise to good ideas; the symbols are too often shrunken, flattened, cute, overcontrolled, merely self-referential, even lying.

Still, I have wanted to continue to join the writer and thinker Suzanne Langer in her call for public symbols capable of "holding and orienting us" in "material and social realities." Capable of giving new grounds for hope. Capable of providing a social context for the healthy functioning of the individual mind.[2] Except that I disagree with Langer's belief that religious communities are too devoted to the petty and the ugly and thus are incapable of setting forth such symbols.

Hoffman has devoted his life precisely to the work of recovering a strong public symbolism—classic yet self-critical—in Jewish homes and synagogues and lives. I am so grateful to him for that work. I have hoped throughout my career to bring similar gifts to my own Evangelical Lutheran Church.

But how does such symbolism "hold and orient us"; how does it interpret our world—indeed, how does it *give* us a world—and enable the recovery of a wide-ranging hope? An example: I have learned from Hoffman how the Mishnah (rabbinic Judaism's formative legal work) articulates the central principle of the Passover Haggadah. According to Hoffman, the seder ritual begins with degradation and ends with praise, concluding with a blessing of redemption.[3] That is amazing. It means that any person participating in the network of enacted symbols that makes up the seder, when the seder is enacted with beauty and integrity—with "emotion, intellect, and artistry," as Hoffman writes—can discover reference to all the degradation with which the world is so full. Not just the narrated degradation of Israel in Egypt, but also, as symbolized by that narrative, all the sorrow and misery and unjust suffering that trouble our world, including the participants' own suffering. But the full ritual also draws the awareness of those sorrows into the awareness of the mystery of God in the world, making possible for the participants a rebirth of hope. The ritual "holds" us, affirming our lived experiences and the possibilities we may encounter. The Passover seder gives its participants a way to walk in the world, a way to stand beside others, a way to encounter degradation and then work again for justice. The ritual orients us. It is not that the seder presents a specific social program or agenda. Indeed, this ritual is not a program; nor is it an entertainment. Rather, it tells the truth about suffering and yet also about God's mercy and the community's joy. It gives ideas in a social context to the individual mind. Ideas. Wrapped in ritual.

I think that the Mishnah's central principle is, in fact, found everywhere in the Bible—in the *Tanach* but also in the Christian canon. Degradation and praise, blessing of God for redemption—these are the basic biblical themes. Christians generally call them "judgment and mercy." Lutherans also call them "law and gospel." They are present in the Bible not as a single, ruling ideology but as symbols variously expressing, through narratives and poetry, law and prophecy, the continuing reality of human sin and sorrow as the context for God's promise and God's redemption. And these biblical symbols do not exist only rolled up in books but also come to us as a network of symbols to be enacted again and again in assembly—in ritual. In Hebrew this is *kahal*; in Greek, *ekklesia*.

Another example: the structure of ritual prayer itself can so hold and orient us. Like Ezekiel's vision of a scroll, such prayer can be full of "lamentations, dirges, and woes" (Ezekiel 2:10) and yet be "as sweet as honey" (Ezekiel 3:3) in the mouth. Classic prayer—think of the fierce lament followed by the communal praise of Psalm 22—unfolds as beseeching from need and thanksgiving for mercy, as a verbal expression of degradation and praise. Or the prayer moves in the opposite direction, as in the thanksgiving and repentance of the prophet Nehemiah, which is immediately followed by beseeching.[4] The double helix of thanksgiving and beseeching, degradation and praise, wrapped around each other and held together in blessing, is the very DNA of prayer. Such a ritual movement holds us, orienting us into hope. The beseeching gives us a way to walk in the world, beholding its need and sorrow, praying for those around us as we walk, enacting our prayer as solidarity. And the thanksgiving also gives a way to walk in the world, ourselves showing the very mercy for which we ourselves long, blessing God for all that is created good, blessing God for every beautiful thing we see.

Of course, ritual must be used critically. A network of enacted symbols can also support bad and destructive ideas, as occurred at Nazi rallies in the 1930s and 1940s or, more recently, at symbolically drenched acts of political insurrection like the events of January 6, 2021. Nonetheless, I rejoice in the growing awareness that biblical symbols themselves—indeed, any religious symbols—must be read critically and then used ritually with what Paul Ricoeur, again, calls "second naiveté."[5] Then the ritual rightly goes on: symbols that we work to make yet better, symbols that hold and orient us in a needy time, rituals that clothe ideas.

So used, healthy and strong ritual can indeed lead to a reemergence of hope and can help us all to "act as if all good things are possible."

CHAPTER 33

Ideas That Matter, Still

Margaret Moers Wenig

Margaret Moers Wenig is a rabbi and longtime teacher at Hebrew Union College-Jewish Institute of Religion in New York City.

Was it the expectation that Jewish worship must offer consolation that motivated a rabbi on Rosh Hashanah 1939 to preach these words?

> If our hearts be saddened this night at the turn of European events, let not our spirits of faith and hope remain unshaken. The darkness now descending upon the face of the earth is but the twilight sleep of an expectant motherhood, the cry of anguish we now hear represents the travail of the earth ere she give life to a new-born civilization. Even in our day we shall behold the children of that coming civilization standing, as if on a bridge, suspended aloft by great cables spun from the golden strands of peace and liberty, who will look on dictator skulls and concentration-camp debris floating toward the sea. A civilization whose children will look down on godlessness passing by and will then look up and see God.[1]

My faith *is* shaken, by new and by seemingly intractable conflicts around the world and by suffering in my own country, where children do not "stand . . . suspended aloft by great cables spun from the golden strands of peace and liberty" but rather lie murdered in their classrooms, in the streets, even in their apartments. "Godlessness" has not "passed by," but rather persists in hate acts and speech we witness daily.

I wish I shared Martin Luther King Jr.'s faith that "the arc of the moral universe... bends towards justice."[2] Perhaps it will. Though in my day, grave injustices persist and some hard-won forms of justice are being dismantled. I wish I could "act as if all good things are possible, as if the Messianic Age is just around the corner." Perhaps Rabbi Larry Hoffman himself would no longer write those words, penned nearly thirty years ago.

Ideas still matter to me. Prayer still matters. Sermons matter. Words of consolation don't. I bristle when leaders of prayer or preachers make promises that are not in their power to fulfill. I don't pray, "Those who sow in tears *will* reap in joy" (Psalm 126:5). I pray, "*May* those who sow in tears reap in joy." I don't declare, "On Rosh Hashanah it *is* written, on Yom Kippur it is sealed." I pray, "On Rosh Hashanah would that [the limits of our lives] be written. Would that they be sealed on Yom Kippur,"[3] rather than by distracted drivers or young men with semiautomatic rifles. Nightly in prayer I voice fears of "enemy and pestilence, sword, famine, and grief."[4]

Jewish particularism, either as God's witnesses or as victims, no longer strikes me as one of our most valuable ideas. In the past, Jews without power may have enjoyed the illusion of a unique claim to righteousness; Jews with power, news reports repeatedly confirm, can be as unjust as other nations and individuals. To be sure, the promise that through Abraham "all the families of the earth [would] be blessed" (Genesis 12:3) has been realized to the extent that Jews have indeed contributed valuable ideas, culture, and science to the world. Yet, the uniqueness suggested by the notion that Israel should be a "light to the nations" (Isaiah 42:6) ignores the manifold ways in which *other* peoples too have enlightened the nations. And rather than compete for greatest-victim status, I acknowledge, with the Reform movement's 1978 Yom Kippur liturgy, "The earth's crust is soaked with the tears of the innocent."[5]

Claims to know God's will, to attribute any event to God's agency, are untenable for me. I argued with the Orthodox rabbi who claimed in a sermon that the shooting at the Tree of Life synagogue had been God's will, that *everything* that happens is an expression of God's will. Were he alone in this, I would not single him out. But in Reform sermons and prayer books, too, not to mention the Torah, claims to know God's past, present, or future actions proliferate. I give thanks before every meal, before sleep, and throughout the day in scripted and spontaneous prayer. In my heart,

I do not credit God for the blessings I enjoy any more than I credit God for the pain I've suffered. (How could I explain that God blessed *me* with sufficient nutrition while others remain without?)

Yet, I still pray and study Torah, for I find in them teachings that urge:

- We treat all people in such a way that "each may come to know they are [as worthy as if] created by God,"[6] while at the same time,
- We eschew affiliation with "evil companions,"[7] those who have "amassed wealth [or power] through unjust, exploitative means" (Jeremiah 17:11), even if such affiliation would bring us personal benefit.
- We resist unjust orders as Egyptian midwives defied their king's order to kill Israelite boys (Exodus 1:17), and we endeavor to over-turn unjust laws.
- We promote a world in which "when a man or woman [a people or a nation] commit a sin . . . they confess their sin . . . and make restitution . . . in full plus an added fifth" (Numbers 5:6–7).
- We endeavor to decrease or "cease the destruction wrought by our hands"[8] upon others and upon the earth, so that future generations might have some chance of living "like a tree planted by waters, sending forth roots by a stream . . . not fearing the coming of heat . . . not fearing drought" (Jeremiah 17:8).
- We drink deeply of the arts, so that even in the midst of a "mean world . . . dark with cruelty,"[9] we may "enlarge the site of our tents" (Isaiah 54:2), broaden the range of our vision, "lengthen the ropes and reinforce the tent pegs" (Isaiah 54:2), to strengthen our resilience and sustain our souls. As one of the prisoners, who performed Verdi's *Requiem* in Theresienstadt using a single smuggled score, testified, "Being in the choir . . . was soul-saving. I survived the war and I still have a soul."[10]
- We study. Given the messiness of human history, ambiguities of causes and effects, uncertain and unintended outcomes, and con-flicting worldviews, reasoned argument in light of changing cir-cumstances and current knowledge still matter.

- As we "walk the world of slaughter,"[11] I no longer speak of "repairing the world," which strikes me as unreachable. But these ideas matter to me still:

  This is the fast I desire:
  To [endeavor to] unlock fetters of wickedness,
  And untie cords of the yoke . . .
  To share your bread with those who are hungry,
  And to take wretched poor into your home.
  When you see the naked, to clothe them,
  And not ignore your own kin. (Isaiah 58:6–8)[12]

  Let not the wise . . . glory in [their] wisdom;
  Let not the strong . . . glory in [their] strength;
  Let not the rich . . . glory in [their] riches;
  But only in this should one glory:
  In . . . earnest devotion to . . .
  compassion, justice, and equity in the world.[13]

NOTES

PREFACE

1 Lawrence Hoffman, *One Hundred Great Jewish Books* (Katonah, NY: BlueBridge, 2011), xii.

FOREWORD (BALIN)

1 Unless otherwise noted, all quotations are from the author's interview with Lawrence A. Hoffman, June 17, 2022.

2 Thomas Kuhn, *The Structure of Scientific Revolutions* (Chicago: University of Chicago Press, 1962). Kuhn held that science experiences periods of stable growth punctuated by revisionary revolutions.

3 Peter L. Berger and Thomas Luckmann, *The Social Construction of Reality: A Treatise in the Sociology of Knowledge* (New York: Anchor Books, 1966). Berger and Luckmann argued that social realities are constructed and maintained in social interaction. That is, we do not find or discover knowledge or reality so much as construct it to make sense of our experiences.

4 Mircea Eliade, *The Sacred and the Profane: The Nature of Religion*, trans. Willard R. Trask (New York: Harvest, Brace & World, 1957). Eliade observed that even moderns who proclaim to be inhabitants of a wholly "profane" or secular world are subconsciously nourished by memory of the sacred.

5 Babylonian Talmud, *M'nachot* 29b.

6 https://www12.statcan.gc.ca/census-recensement/2021/dp-pd/dv-vd/ribbon -ruban/index-eng.cfm.

7 Rabbi Stephen S. Wise, the renowned advocate of social justice, founded the Jewish Institute of Religion (JIR) in 1922 in New York City as a nondenominational rabbinical seminary. It merged with Hebrew Union College (HUC) in 1950. See Shirley Idelson, *We Shall Build Anew: Stephen S. Wise, the Jewish Institute of Religion, and the Reinvention of American Judaism* (Tuscaloosa: University of Alabama Press, 2022).

8 Victor Turner, "Betwixt and Between: The Liminal Period in Rites of Passage," in *The Forest of Symbols: Aspects of Ndembu Ritual* (Ithaca and London: Cornell University Press, 1967), 93–111. Victor Turner—and his research partner, unacknowledged co-author, and wife, Edith—developed the notion of liminality (from the Latin *limen*, "threshold"), coined by the folklorist Arnold van Gennep in 1909. The Turners understood liminality as a state of ambiguity, openness, and indeterminacy describing the middle stage of a rite of passage.

9 Lawrence A. Hoffman, "A Rabbinic *Berakhah* and Jewish Spirituality," in *Asking and Thanking*, ed. Christian Duquoc and Castano Florestan (Philadelphia: Trinity Press, 1990), 18–30.

FOREWORD (Zemel)

1 Louis Newman, "Woodchoppers and Respirators: The Problem of Interpretation in Contemporary Jewish Ethics" in *Modern Judaism*, vol. 10 (Oxford University Press, 1990): 17-42.

2 Jürgen Habermas, *An Awareness of What is Missing: Faith and Reason in a Post-Secular Age* (Cambridge: Polity, 2010).

3 Masha Gessen, *Surviving Autocracy* (New York: Random House, 2021).

4 Lawrence A. Hoffman, "The Once and Future Synagogue: Fifty Years of Temple Micah and Its Thirty Years with Rabbi Zemel," an address presented at Temple Micah, Washington, DC, June 2013.

CHAPTER 1

1 Elaine Scarry, *On Beauty and Being Just* (Princeton: Princeton University Press, 1998).

2 Scarry, *On Beauty*, 80–86.

3 Scarry, *On Beauty*, 3.

4 Scarry, *On Beauty*, 23.

5 Scarry, *On Beauty*, 29.

6 Janet Walton, *Art and Worship: A Vital Connection* (Collegeville, MN: Liturgical, 1988), 60.

7 Walton, *Art and Worship*, 81.

8 Scarry, *On Beauty*, 46.

9 Liturgical art is art that tells our story—whatever "telling," "our," and "story" might mean at any given moment. It is art that affirms our theology—whichever theology we want to call "ours." It is art that laments our brokenness and the brokenness of our world. It is art that confesses our shortcomings and expresses our yearning for healing. It is art that praises what is good, wise, beautiful, and true in this world.

CHAPTER 2

1 Jed Pearl, *Authority and Freedom: In Defense of the Arts* (New York: Knopf Doubleday, 2022), 14.

2 From Rabbi Peter Rubinstein's sermon: https://www.centralsynagogue.org/worship/sermons/catching-up-to-prophets-rosh-hashanah-5777

CHAPTER 3

1 See Genesis 25:29–34.

SECTION 2

1 Martin Buber, *Ten Rungs*, trans. Olga Marx (London: Routledge, 2002), 52.

CHAPTER 4

1   Mark Zborowski and Elizabeth Herzog, *Life Is with People: The Culture of the Shtetl* (New York: Schocken Books, 1995).

CHAPTER 5

1   Babylonian Talmud, *B'rachot* 31a

CHAPTER 6

1   Ron Wolfson and Steven Windmueller, "The Rise of the Online Synagogue," *Tablet*, April 6, 2022.
2   Wolfson and Windmueller, "The Rise of the Online Synagogue."
3   Wolfson and Windmueller, "The Rise of the Online Synagogue."
4   Percival Goodman, "Modern Artist as Synagogue Builder: Satisfying the Needs of Today's Congregations," *Commentary*, June 1949, 51–55.
5   Lawrence A. Hoffman, "Sacred Space: The Message of Design," in *The Art of Public Prayer: Not for Clergy Only*, 2nd ed. (Woodstock, VT: SkyLight Paths, 1999), 194.
6   Sources are found in the study of proxemics, territoriality, distance factors, lighting design, color psychology, ergonomics, anthropometrics, and architecture.
7   Aaron Spiegel and Lawrence A. Hoffman, *2020 FACT Survey of Reform and Conservative Congregations* (Indianapolis: Synagogue Studies Institute, 2022), 11–12.

CHAPTER 7

1   *Mishnah Sanhedrin* 4:5.
2   *Pirkei DeRabbi Eliezer* 11:5-6.
3   Pew Research Center, *Jewish Americans in 2020*, (Washington, DC: Pew Research Center, May 11, 2021), 11, 47.
4   Pew Research Center, *Jewish Americans in 2020*, 39.
5   https://www.respectability.org/2014/06/new-poll-data-of-2607-jews-these-jews-feel-strongly-about-inclusion-of-people-with-disabilities-even-more-so-than-israel-jewish-life-marrying-jewish-or-having-jewish-kids/.
6   https://www.respectability.org/2014/06/new-poll-data-of-2607-jews-these-jews-feel-strongly-about-inclusion-of-people-with-disabilities-even-more-so-than-israel-jewish-life-marrying-jewish-or-having-jewish-kids/.

SECTION 3

1   Philip Birnbaum, ed. and trans., *High Holiday Prayer Book* (New York: Hebrew Publishing Company, 2002), 490, quoted in Deborrah Cannizzaro, "A Brief History of the Kol Nidrei Prayer," *ReformJudaism.org* (blog), September 17, 2018, https://reformjudaism.org/blog/brief-history-kol-nidrei-prayer.

CHAPTER 9

1   Lawrence Hoffman, *Beyond the Text: A Holistic Approach to Liturgy* (Bloomington: Indiana University Press, 1987), 2.

2   Hoffmann, *Beyond the Text*, 7.

3   *Zohar* 3:152a; Moses Cordovero, *Pardes rimonim* 5:4, 25d, cited in Daniel C. Matt, *The Essential Kabbalah: The Heart of Jewish Mysticism* (San Francisco: HarperSanFrancisco, 1995), 91.

4   Lawrence A. Hoffman, *The Art of Public Prayer: Not for Clergy Only* (Woodstock, VT: SkyLight Paths, 1999), 166.

5   Marianne Moore, "Poetry," in *The Norton Anthology of Modern Poetry*, ed. Richard Ellmann and Robert O'Clair (New York: W.W. Norton, 1973), 421.

6   Elisa Gabbert, "On Poetry," *New York Times Book Review*, April 17, 2022, 9.

CHAPTER 10

1   In his essay, "How Ritual Means: Ritual Circumcision in Rabbinic Culture and Today," *Studia Liturgica* 23, no. 1 (1993): 78–97, Hoffman mentions another layer, the normative meaning.

SECTION 4

1   The actual exchange from Lewis Carroll's *Alice's Adventures in Wonderland* (available as an e-book at https://www.gutenberg.org/files/11/11-h/11-h.htm) begins with Alice's saying, "Would you tell me, please, which way I ought to go from here?" It continues:
"That depends a good deal on where you want to get to," said the Cat.
"I don't much care where—" said Alice.
"Then it doesn't matter which way you go," said the Cat.
"—so long as I get *somewhere*," Alice added as an explanation.
"Oh, you're sure to do that," said the Cat, "if you only walk long enough."

2   Douglas discussed and refined this model over two decades. An early source is Mary Douglas, *Natural Symbols: Explorations in Cosmology* (London: Barrie & Rockliff, 1970). See also Douglas, *Essays in the Sociology of Perception* (London: Routledge & Kegan Paul, 1982).

3   See, e.g., Mary Douglas and Aaron Wildavsky, *Risk and Culture: An Essay on the Selection of Technical and Environmental Dangers* (Berkeley: University of California Press, 1982), esp. 9.

CHAPTER 11

1   For more on these themes, see Andrew Rehfeld, "A Non-Bifurcated Engagement with Torah," TheTorah.com, 2022, https://thetorah.com/article/a-non-bifurcated-engagement-with-torah.

2   Benedict R. Anderson, *Imagined Communities: Reflections on the Origin and Spread of Nationalism* (London: Verso, 1983).

CHAPTER 12

1   The passage is available as Solomon Schechter, "The History of an Idea," in *Tradition and Change: The Development of Conservative Judaism*, ed. Mordechai Waxman (New York: Burning Bush Press, 1958), 94. It first appeared in *First Studies in Judaism*, published in 1896.
2   Schechter, "History of an Idea," 94.
3   Solomon Schechter, "His Majesty's Opposition," in *Seminary Addresses and Other Papers* (New York, Burning Bush, 1959), 240.
4   Solomon Schechter, "The Seminary as Witness," in *Seminary Addresses*, 51–52.
5   Schechter, "History of an Idea," 94.

CHAPTER 13

1   Mordecai M. Kaplan, *Religion as Ethical Nationhood* (New York: Macmillan, 1970), 4–5.
2   Kaplan made this statement in many works. See, e.g., Mordecai Kaplan, *Not So Random Thoughts* (New York: Reconstructionist Press, 1966), 263.

CHAPTER 14

1   "Report on the Special Committee Appointed to Study and Recommend What Steps Should Be Taken with Respect to the Growth of the Congregation, and How Best the Problem of Reform Judaism in Kansas City Can Be Met," *Board Minutes of Congregation B'nai Jehudah*, January 11, 1958, American Jewish Archives.
2   "Judaism on Rise in Suburbs," *New York Times*, April 5, 1959, 1.
3   See, e.g., the 2015 Boston Jewish Community Survey, which showed a rising number of members in "alternative" synagogues such as minyanim and a declining number of families in traditional denominational synagogues: https://scholarworks.brandeis.edu/esploro/outputs/report/2015-Greater-Boston-Jewish-Community-Study/9924088245601921#file-0.
4   Peter Berger, *The Many Altars of Modernity: Toward a Paradigm for Religion in a Pluralistic Age* (Boston: De Gruyter, 2014), 45.
5   See the Public Religion Research Institute's *2020 Census of American Religion* on the slight rise in mainline Protestants between 2018 and 2020: https://www.prri.org/research/2020-census-of-american-religion/#page-section-1.

CHAPTER 16

1   At The Kitchen, we choose not to capitalize the words "god," "shabbat," and "torah," so as to make them more integrated into our everyday language.
2   See *Targum Jonathan* on Exodus 26:28; *Midrash Tanchuma, T'rumah* 9:14; *Sh'mot Rabbah* 33:8.
3   See for example Heschel's essay on prayer, "Choose Life!," *Jubilee*, vol. 13, no. 9 (January 1966), pp. 37-39.

CHAPTER 17

1   Simon Rawidowicz, *Studies in Jewish Thought*, ed. Nahum N. Glatzer (Philadelphia: Jewish Publication Society, 1964), 223.

2   Conrad Hackett and Jacob Ausubel, "Measuring the Size of the U.S. Jewish Population: New Estimates from a Pew Research Center Survey of Jewish Americans," *Journal of Religion and Demography* 8 (2021): 93.

3   Pew Research Center, *Jewish Americans in 2020* (Washington, DC: Pew Research Center, 2021), 93–94; Jonathan D. Sarna, *American Judaism: A History*, 2nd ed. (New Haven: Yale University Press, 2019), 363.

4   For the report commissioned by the Union for Reform Judaism on its past experience and response to sexual harassment and abuse, see https://urj.org/sites/default/files/2022-02/URJ_Investigation_Report.pdf. For the HUC-JIR report, see http://huc.edu/sites/default/files/About/PDF/HUC%20REPORT%20OF%20INVESTIGATION%20--%2011.04.21.pdf.

5   Drorah Setel, "Debbie Friedman's Healing Prayer," *Forward*, January 19, 2011, https://forward.com/opinion/134774/debbie-friedman-s-healing-prayer/).

6   Lance J. Sussman, "The Hidden Battle for the Soul of Reform Judaism," eJewish Philanthropy, March 31, 2022, https://ejewishphilanthropy.com/the-hidden-battle-for-the-soul-of-reform-judaism/.

CHAPTER 18

1   Rashi on *B'reishit Rabbah* 56:2.

2   United Jewish Communities, *National Jewish Population Survey 2000–1* (New York: United Jewish Communities, 2003).

3   *M'chilta d'Rabbi Yishmael*, Exodus 19:2.

4   Leo Baeck, *This People Israel: The Meaning of Jewish Existence* (New York: Holt, Rinehart, & Winston, Union of American Hebrew Congregations, 1964), 393.

CHAPTER 19

1   Claudio Carvalhaes, *Liturgies from Below: Praying with People at the End of the World* (Nashville, TN: Abingdon, 2020), 21.

2   Carvalhaes, *Liturgies from Below*, 19.

3   Carvalhaes, *Liturgies from Below*, 290.

4   Sally F. Moore and Barbara G. Meyerhoff, eds., *Secular Ritual* (Amsterdam: Van Gorcum, 1977), 22.

5   Carvalhaes, *Liturgies from Below*, 22.

6   Abraham Joshua Heschel, "Depth-Theology," *Cross Currents* 10, no. 4 (Fall 1960): 317–25.

SECTION 7

1   Richard Rorty, *Contingency, Irony, and Solidarity* (Cambridge: Cambridge University Press 1989), 7.

CHAPTER 20

1 Robert Grosseteste, *Chateau d'Amour* (London: J. R. Smith, 1852), 2.
2 All translations are my own.
3 *M'chilta d'Rabbi Yishmael* 20:15.
4 *M'chilta d'Rabbi Yishmael* 20:1.
5 *M'chilta d'Rabbi Yishmael* 20:8.
6 *Sh'mot Rabbah* 28:6.

CHAPTER 21

1 Lawrence Hoffman, "The State of Things," paper presented at Responding to This Moment in the American Jewish Experience: A Conversation, Temple Micah, Washington, DC, December 2019.
2 Alan Mittleman, *Human Nature and Jewish Thought: Judaism's Case for Why Persons Matter* (Princeton: Princeton University Press, 2015), 18–19.

SECTION 8

1 Clifford Geertz, *The Interpretation of Cultures* (New York: Basic Books, 1973), 10.

CHAPTER 23

1 Tony Bayfield, *Being Jewish Today: Confronting the Real Issues* (London: Bloomsbury, 2019).
2 *Forms of Prayer*, vol. 1 (1977, 2008); vol. 2 (1995); vol. 3 (1985) (London: Reform Synagogues of Great Britain).
3 I have used the idiom "front line" advisedly. Not only are there conflicts—often creative—within the leadership of synagogues over the way forward, but synagogues are on the front line of the struggle with secularism, religious fundamentalism, and, no less a challenge, the trivialization of Judaism.
4 *Pirkei Avot* 5:20. Here a distinction is made between creative disagreements that seek to further our understanding and disagreements that stem from personal ambition.

CHAPTER 24

1 Author's translation.
2 Mount Sinai (where Moses received Revelation) and Mount Horeb (where Elijah experiences God's presence) are considered by both the Bible and rabbinic tradition to be one and the same.
3 Author's translation.
4 *Sh'mot Rabbah* 29:9, adapted from the Soncino translation.
5 Judith Plaskow, *Standing Again at Sinai: Judaism from a Feminist Perspective* (New York: HarperCollins, 1990), 56. Plaskow, like the ancient rabbis, was writing for her own time; thirty years later, we can add to this quotation by considering other marginalized genders and identities as well.

CHAPTER 26

1 *Siddur Pirchei Kodesh*, (Toronto: Holy Blossom Temple, 2011).
2 Babylonian Talmud, *Yoma* 69b.
3 Babylonian Talmud, *Megillah* 25a.

CHAPTER 27

1 Babylonian Talmud, *M'nachot* 29b.

SECTION 10

1 Susan Sontag, *Illness as Metaphor* (New York: Farrar, Straus, & Giroux, 1978), 3.
2 Annie Dillard, *Living by Fiction* (New York: Harper and Row, 1982; Perennial Library ed., 1988), 137–39.
3 See Susan Sontag, "Against Interpretation," in *Against Interpretation, and Other Essays*, (New York: Farrar, Straus, & Giroux, 1966), 13–23.
4 Ludwig Wittgenstein, *Tractatus Logico-Philosophicus*, trans. C. K. Ogden (London: Routledge & Kegan Paul, 1922), 6.522.
5 Ludwig Wittgenstein, *Lectures and Conversations on Aesthetics, Psychology, and Religious Beliefs*, comp. from notes taken by Yorick Smythies, Rush Rhees, and James Taylor, ed. Cyril Barrett, 2nd ed. (Berkeley: University of California Press, 2007), 55.

CHAPTER 28

1 The phrase "foretaste of the world to come" is from A. J. Heschel, *The Sabbath* (New York: Farrar, Straus and Giroux, 1951), 74. "Dreamers" upon returning to the Promised Land, comes from Psalm 126:1, which begins the Grace After Meals on Shabbat. "By the waters of Babylon" from Psalm 137:1, begins the Grace After Meals on weekdays.

CHAPTER 29

1 Susan Sontag, *Illness as Metaphor* (New York: Farrar, Straus, & Giroux, 1978), 3.
2 Ellen Samuels, "Six Ways of Looking at Crip Time," *Disability Studies Quarterly* 37, no. 3, unpaginated, https://dsq-sds.org/article/view/5824/4684.
3 Samuels, "Six Ways," unpaginated.

CHAPTER 30

1 All biblical translations in this essay are my own.
2 See Franz Rosenzweig, *Zeit ists: Gedanken über jüdischen Bildungsproblem des Augenblicks. An Hermann Cohen*, 2nd ed. (Berlin: Verlag der Neuen Jüdischen Monatshefte, 1918).
3 Martin Luther King Jr., "Remaining Awake through a Great Revolution" (speech, National Cathedral, Washington, DC, March 31, 1968).

CHAPTER 31

1   Samuel David Luzzatto, "Letter to Michael Sachs" [in Hebrew], in *Iggerot Shadal*, vol. 2 (Josef Fischer, 1891), 778ff.

2   Clifford Geertz, *The Interpretation of Cultures: Selected Essays* (New York: Basic Books, 1973), 5.

3   Robert Cover, "The Folktales of Justice: Tales of Jurisdiction," *Capital University Law Review* 14 (1984–85): 182.

4   Cover, "Folktales of Justice," 182.

5   Ronald Garet, "Meaning and Ending," *Yale Law Journal* 96 (1987): 1823.

CHAPTER 32

1   Paul Ricoeur, *The Symbolism of Evil*, trans. Emerson Buchanan (Boston: Beacon Press, 1967), 347.

2   Suzanne K. Langer, *Philosophy in a New Key: A Study in the Symbolism of Reason, Rite and Art* (Cambridge, MA: Harvard University Press, 1942), 288–89.

3   *Mishnah P'sachim* 10.

4   Nehemiah 9:6–37 (with the turn from thanksgiving and repentance to beseeching at 9:32).

5   Ricoeur, *Symbolism of Evil*, 352.

CHAPTER 33

1   Sermon by Rabbi Abraham H. Feinberg, Temple Beth-El, Rockford, IL, in Marc Saperstein, *Jewish Preaching in Times of War, 1800–2001* (Oxford: Littman Library of Jewish Civilization, 2008), 198.

2   Martin Luther King Jr., "Remaining Awake through a Great Revolution" (speech, National Cathedral, Washington, DC, March 31, 1968).

3   In both cases, the verbs are in the imperfect tense, not in the present tense! The imperfect can be translated either as the certain future or as the wished-for future, as in "May God bless you and keep you." That is how I understand these verbs.

4   In Hashkiveinu, the final blessing of the *Sh'ma* and Its Blessings, here trans. Philip Birnbaum, ed. and trans., *High Holiday Prayer Book* (New York: Hebrew Publishing Company, 1951), 28.

5   *Shaarei Teshuvah/Gates of Repentance: The New Union Prayerbook for the Days of Awe* (New York: Central Conference of American Rabbis, 1978), 430.

6   From M'loch, the emblematic prayer of the Rosh Hashanah K'dushat Hayom, in *Mishkan HaNefesh: Machzor for the Days of Awe*, vol. 1, *Rosh Hashanah* (New York: CCAR Press, 2015), 56.

7   Ben Zion Bokser, ed. and trans., *The Prayer Book: Weekday, Sabbath and Festival* (New York: Hebrew Publishing Company, 1957), 6.

8   In Atah Notein Yad and Atah Hivdalta, two of the key prayers of the N'ilah service of Yom Kippur, we articulate the purpose of our whole process of repentance. It's not to earn ourselves another year of life, but *l'ma'an nechdal mei'oshek yadeinu*, "to cease/refrain from the harm we cause with our own hands," or, in the

words of the current Reform prayer book for Yom Kippur, "to turn our hands into instruments of good, to cause no harm or oppression." See *Mishkan HaNefesh: Machzor for the Days of Awe*, vol. 2, *Yom Kippur* (New York: CCAR Press, 2015), 654.

9 Maya Angelou, "Continue," in *Celebrations: Rituals of Peace and Prayer* (New York: Random House, 2006). I thank Rabbi Tamar Malino for introducing me to this poem.

10 Bryony Clarke, "The Concentration Camp Choir," Opinion, *Wall Street Journal*, Aug. 2, 2018.

11 The expression comes from a poem by Chaim Nachman Bialik, "Ir Haharega" ("The City of Slaughter"). These words are adapted from an English translation by Helena Frank of the Yiddish version of part of Bialik's poem; they appear in *Shaarei Teshuvah/Gates of Repentance*, 436.

12 Part of the Yom Kippur morning haftarah.

13 My own adaptation of Jeremiah 9:23, based on *Tanakh/The Holy Scriptures: The New JPS Translation according to the Traditional Hebrew Text* (Philadelphia: Jewish Publication Society, 1985).

Jill Abramson is the director of the Debbie Friedman School of Sacred Music at Hebrew Union College-Jewish Institute of Religion in New York. She previously served congregations in Scarsdale, New York; Greenwich, Connecticut; and Chicago. She is a passionate teacher, with specializations in the intersection of the arts and Jewish life, as well as in women's leadership and learning. She is also committed to international social justice work, having created an Israeli and Arab teenage choir as part of an international peace program, and has lived and taught in Cameroon and Indonesia. She holds a BA in Anthropology from Grinnell College and a Master of Sacred Music, and was ordained a cantor by HUC-JIR.

Carole B. Balin is a prolific writer and teacher known for her fresh ideas, authenticity, and way with words. She is chair of the board of the Jewish Women's Archive and professor emerita of history at her alma mater, Hebrew Union College–Jewish Institute of Religion, where she was the first woman at the New York campus to earn tenure. A Phi Beta Kappa graduate of Wellesley College, she earned a doctorate at Columbia University and speaks and publishes widely on gender and the Jewish experience. Balin is currently writing a book about bat mitzvah anchored in the stories of the pioneering girls who sparked a gender revolution in Jewish life. Her work on the Jewish coming-of-age rite has been featured on NPR's *All Things Considered* and in the *New York Times*, the *Forward*, and additional media outlets.

Tony Bayfield was born in London, read law at Cambridge, and received *s'michah* from Leo Baeck College. He was the founding rabbi of North West Surrey Synagogue, first director of the Sternberg Centre for Judaism in North West London, and from 1983 to 2011, founder editor of the journal *MANNA*. From 1995 to 2010, he was chief executive, then professional head of the Movement for Reform Judaism in Britain. He is professor emeritus of Jewish theology and thought at Leo Baeck College.

A leading figure in the methodology and theology of dialogue between the Abrahamic faiths, he is responsible for four books. He is only the third Jew ever to have received a doctorate in divinity from the Archbishop of Canterbury. Bayfield has three children, one of whom is a senior Reform rabbi in Finchley, London.

Joshua I. Beraha is an associate rabbi at Temple Micah in Washington, DC, where he has served since 2014. He has a BA in History and Hebrew Literature from the University of Wisconsin-Madison and an MA in Education through the New York City Teaching Fellows Program. He spent five years teaching students with special needs at a public school on the Lower East Side of Manhattan.

Angela Warnick Buchdahl serves as the senior rabbi of Central Synagogue in New York City, a flagship Reform synagogue, dubbed the first "mega-shul" by the *Wall Street Journal*. She is the first woman to lead Central in its 180-year history. Born in Seoul, Korea, Buchdahl graduated from Yale University and went on to become the first Asian American ordained as a cantor and rabbi by Hebrew Union College–Jewish Institute of Religion. She has been nationally recognized for her innovations in leading worship, which draw large crowds in the congregation's historic sanctuary and live streamers in more than one hundred countries. In 2014, President Barak Obama invited her to share blessings and light the menorah for the White House Hanukkah Party. She has been featured on the *Today Show*, NPR, PBS, and *Newsweek*'s "America's 50 Most Influential Rabbis." Buchdahl and her husband, Jacob, have three children.

Joshua M. Davidson holds the Peter and Mary Kalikow Senior Rabbinic Chair of Congregation Emanu-El of the City of New York. He previously served at Temple Beth El in Chappaqua, New York, and Central Synagogue in New York City. Davidson is a graduate of Princeton University and was ordained by Hebrew Union College–Jewish Institute of Religion (HUC-JIR), and his work has included anti-death penalty advocacy, LGBTQ inclusion, and interfaith dialogue. He is active in rabbinic leadership, including the HUC-JIR Board of Governors, HUC-JIR's President's Rabbinic Council, and UJA-Federation of New York and as chair of A Partnership of Faith in New York City. His articles have appeared in *Commentary*, the *New York Times*, *New York Post*, *Jerusalem Post*, and *Huffington Post*. He is a contributing writer in Rabbi Larry Hoffman's Prayers of Awe series.

Arnold M. Eisen is chancellor emeritus and professor of Jewish thought at the Jewish Theological Seminary. A leading expert on Jewish religious thought and practice in the modern period, with particular focus on the United States and Israel, Eisen is the author (among other works) of *Galut: Modern Jewish Reflection on Homelessness and Homecoming*, *Rethinking Modern Judaism: Ritual, Commandment, Community*, and (with Steven M. Cohen) *The Jew Within: Self, Family and Community in America*. He is currently at work on an essay in personal theology.

David H. Ellenson is chancellor emeritus of Hebrew Union College–Jewish Institute of Religion, where he served as president from 2001 to 2013 and again during 2018–19. He is also a past director of the Schusterman Center for Israel Studies and professor emeritus of Near Eastern and Judaic studies at Brandeis University. Rabbi Ellenson has been a student, friend, and colleague of Rabbi Larry Hoffman for fifty years.

Jodie M. Gordon is a rabbi at Hevreh of Southern Berkshire, a Reform congregation in Great Barrington, Massachusetts, where she has served since her ordination from Hebrew Union College–Jewish Institute of Religion. She earned her BA from Brandeis University. She grew up with strong connections in the Reform movement, especially through her time at URJ Eisner Camp, which instilled in her a lifelong love for Jewish learning and the Berkshires. Her path to the rabbinate was paved with invaluable experiences in a variety of Jewish communal institutions, including the Hillel at the University of Wisconsin, the JCC in Manhattan, and Ma'yan: The Jewish Women's Project. She is part of the Tisch Rabbinical Fellowship Alumni program of HUC-JIR. She is also the co-host of the *OMfG Podcast: Jewish Wisdom for Unprecedented Times*. Gordon and her husband, Josh, are the proud parents of two children, who are consistently the greatest teachers she has ever had.

Sarah Grabiner was ordained by Hebrew Union College–Jewish Institute of Religion's Debbie Friedman School of Sacred Music in New York in 2019 and enjoyed the opportunity to study there with Rabbi Larry Hoffman, both in the classroom and as a Tisch-Star fellow. She took up her current role as the assistant director of the Year in Israel Program at HUC-JIR in Jerusalem after serving as the cantor of Radlett Reform Synagogue just outside London in the UK. In addition to her cantorial education, she has studied Hebrew as an undergraduate at Oxford University and has a master's degree in theoretical linguistics from University College London. She is currently undertaking her doctoral research in the Hebrew and Jewish Studies Department at UCL, studying liturgy, translation, and linguistics.

Lisa J. Grushcow is the senior rabbi of Temple Emanu-El-Beth Sholom, the sole Reform synagogue in Montreal and Quebec. Previously she served as associate rabbi at Congregation Rodeph Sholom in New York City. A Rhodes Scholar and Wexner Graduate Fellow, she received her doctorate from Oxford University and was ordained by Hebrew Union College–Jewish Institute of Religion. Author of *Writing the Wayward Wife: Rabbinic Interpretations of Sotah* and editor of *The Sacred Encounter: Jewish Perspectives on Sexuality*, she also has contributed to *The Torah: A Women's Commentary*, *The Mussar Torah Commentary*, *Encyclopedia of the Bible and Its Reception*, and other publications in print and online. She is a lifelong student of Rabbi Larry Hoffman and wrote "First Plant the Sapling: Beyond Messianic Leadership" for his book *More Than Managing: The Relentless Pursuit of Effective Jewish Leadership*.

Hilly Haber is the Director of Social Justice Organizing and Education at Central Synagogue in New York City. Rabbi Haber also has taught men and women on Rikers Island through Manhattan College. She and her wife, Rabbi Rachel Marder of Congregation Beth El in South Orange,

New Jersey, are also the rabbinic chaplains at Northern State Prison in Newark. Ordained at Hebrew Union College-Jewish Institute of Religion, Rabbi Haber was a Wexner Graduate Fellow and a Tisch Fellow. Rabbi Haber is pursuing her PhD at Union Theological Seminary.

Joel M. Hoffman is a scholar, author, and popular speaker. He has served on the faculties of Brandeis University and Hebrew Union College-Jewish Institute of Religion, and authored or contributed to more than twenty books, many of them in collaboration with his father. He has lectured about his work on all six inhabitable continents, and hasn't given up on Antarctica.

Delphine Horvilleur is France's third female rabbi and the managing editor of the quarterly Jewish magazine *Tenou'a*. She leads a congregation in Paris, and co-leads the Liberal Jewish Movement of France, a Jewish liberal cultural and religious association affiliated to the World Union for Progressive Judaism.

Daniel A. Judson is the provost of Hebrew College in Newton, Massachusetts. He received his doctorate in Jewish history from Brandeis University and his book *Pennies for Heaven: The History of American Synagogues and Money* was a finalist for the National Jewish Book Award in 2018.

Elliot Kukla (he/they) is an author, visual artist, and activist. He has been tending to grief, dying, and illness since 2007 and engaged in justice work since 1996. In 2006, he was ordained as the first openly transgender rabbi. His writing on disability, climate, and gender justice appears regularly in the *New York Times* and many other publications, and his activism is frequently mentioned in international media. In 2022, he was even a *New Yorker* crossword puzzle clue (April 12, 7 across)! They are currently on the faculty of SVARA, "a traditionally radical yeshiva," where they founded and now direct the Communal Loss Adaptional Project (CLAP). They live in Oakland with their partner, kid, chosen family, a Boston terrier, and a cat named Turkey.

Noa Kushner founded The Kitchen in 2011 in response to friends who were looking for an informal, transformative shabbat experience that they couldn't find. Along the way, she crashed headfirst into what has now been well documented as a generational trend away from many established religious institutions. The Kitchen quickly grew from a local shabbat experiment into an active doorway for San Francisco's Gen X and millennials looking for serious Jewish life. Through an emphasis on firsthand experience and "doing jewish" over pedigree, The Kitchen has become an international resource, growing to serve thousands of modern families in San Francisco and around the world. Kushner was ordained by Hebrew Union College–Jewish Institute of Religion. Her written work appears in many publications including *The Torah: A Women's Commentary* and Rabbi Larry Hoffman's Prayers of Awe series. Kushner is married to Rabbi Michael Lezak, and together they have three daughters.

Gordon W. Lathrop is the Schieren Professor of Liturgy Emeritus at the United Lutheran Seminary (USA) and a pastor in the Evangelical Lutheran Church in America. He has degrees from Occidental College (Los Angeles) and Luther Theological Seminary (St. Paul), a doctorate in New Testament studies from the Radboud University in Nijmegen, the Netherlands, and honorary doctorates in theology from the University of Helsinki, the University of Iceland, the Virginia Theological Seminary, and Wartburg Theological Seminary. He is the author of several books, including *Holy Things: A Liturgical Theology* (Fortress, 1993), *The Four Gospels on Sunday: The New Testament and the Reform of Christian Worship* (Fortress, 2012), *Saving Images: The Presence of the Bible in Christian Liturgy* (Fortress, 2017), and *The Assembly: A Spirituality* (Fortress, 2022). He is a past president of both Societas Liturgica and the North American Academy of Liturgy.

Emily Langowitz is the Jewish Engagement and Learning manager at the Union for Reform Judaism. Prior to her time at the URJ, she served as a rabbi at Temple Solel in Paradise Valley, Arizona. She received ordination and a master's of Hebrew literature from Hebrew Union College–Jewish

Institute of Religion in New York and holds a BA in Modern Hebrew from Yale University. She writes and teaches extensively on Judaism, abortion, and reproductive justice and is deeply committed to crafting rich language and ideas that reflect progressive Judaism in the twenty-first century. Langowitz lives in Phoenix, Arizona, with her wife, Meaghan Kramer, a disability rights attorney.

Liz A. Lerman is a choreographer, writer, educator, and recipient of honors including the MacArthur "Genius Grant," Guggenheim Fellowship, and American Jewish Congress "Golda" Award. At Temple Micah, she partnered with Rabbi Daniel Zemel in building participatory forms of movement, worship, and art. She joyfully collaborated with Rabbi Larry Hoffman on developing creative practices for prayer. Lerman founded and led Dance Exchange from 1976 until 2011. Recent projects include her performance piece *Wicked Bodies*, an exhibition at Yerba Buena Center for the Arts, and building the Atlas of Creative Tools, an online resource for sharing tools across disciplines. She is the author of *Critical Response Process*, *Hiking the Horizontal*, *Teaching Dance to Senior Adults*, and *Critique Is Creative*. She is a fellow at YBCA and at the Center for the Study of Race and Democracy at Arizona State University and a former fellow at the Robert W. Deutsch Foundation. Lerman is currently an institute professor at ASU.

Dalia Marx is the Rabbi Aaron D. Panken Professor of Liturgy and Midrash at Hebrew Union College–Jewish Institute of Religion's Taube Family Campus in Jerusalem and teaches in various academic institutions in Israel and Europe. She is the tenth generation of her family in Jerusalem. Marx writes for academic and popular journals and publications. She is the author of several books and the chief editor of the Israeli Reform siddur, *T'filat HaAdam* (2020). Her book *From Time to Time: Journeys in the Jewish Calendar* (Yediot Sfarim, 2018) was translated into several languages and is currently being translated into English by the CCAR Press.

Dan Medwin is Co-Director of Growth and Innovation at 6 Points Sci-Tech Camp run by the Union for Reform Judaism. Rabbi Medwin worked at the Central Conference of American Rabbis for more than a decade as the Director of Digital Media creating digital liturgy, such as Visual T'filah, apps, and ebooks, as well as providing general technology and media guidance for other Reform rabbis and the broader Reform Movement. He lives with his wife and three children in Atlanta.

Shira I. Milgrom reflects a generation of rabbis who passionately create extraordinary encounters with Jewish texts, rituals, and traditions that merge the intimate and personal with the grand vision of Judaism and the Jewish people. She has been rabbi of Congregation Kol Ami in White Plains, New York, for thirty-seven years. Milgrom has traveled throughout North America bringing Jews closer to the words of Torah and Jewish self-expression. She is a graduate of Hebrew Union College–Jewish Institute of Religion and has academic training in a wide range of learning. She is the author of articles on Jewish spirituality, education, and healing. She is also the editor of a unique siddur now used in settings across the continent. Milgrom is married to Dr. David Elcott, and they have four children and ten grandchildren.

Sonja K. Pilz is the spiritual leader of Congregation Beth Shalom in Bozeman, Montana. She earned her doctorate from the Department of Rabbinic Literature at Potsdam University in Germany and holds rabbinic ordination from Abraham Geiger College in Germany. Prior to Congregation Beth Shalom, she worked for the Central Conference of American Rabbis as editor of CCAR Press. She also taught worship, liturgy, and ritual at Hebrew Union College–Jewish Institute of Religion in New York and the School of Jewish Theology at Potsdam University, and she served as a rabbinic intern, adjunct rabbi, and cantorial soloist for congregations in Germany, Switzerland, Israel, and the United States. Not surprisingly, she loves to write poetry, midrashim, and prayers. Her work has been published in *ERGON*, *Liturgy*, *Worship*, the *CCAR Journal*,

Ritualwell, and a number of anthologies. Pilz lives with her husband and children in Bozeman.

Andrew Rehfeld is the tenth President of Hebrew Union College-Jewish Institute of Religion. His career has bridged the academic and Jewish professional worlds as a tenured faculty member in Political Science at Washington University (2001-2019) and as President and CEO of the Jewish Federation of St. Louis (2012-2019). Author of *The Concept of Constituency* (Cambridge University Press, 2005), his academic research focuses on the intersection of democracy, human rights, justice, and institutional design. Other areas of published research include the history of political thought and the philosophy of the social sciences. Rehfeld earned a PhD in Political Science (2000) and a Master of Public Policy (1994) from the University of Chicago, and a B.A., Phi Beta Kappa, in the Philosophy Honors Program at the University of Rochester (1989). He currently serves as a member of the board of the American Jewish Joint Distribution Committee.

Daniel Reiser is the rabbi of Temple Beth Shalom in Hastings-on-Hudson, New York. He serves on the editorial board of the *CCAR Journal: The Reform Jewish Quarterly*, as well as on the Leadership Council of the Tisch Fellowship Alumni Network. He and his wife, Leah, live with their two daughters in Westchester, New York.

Nicole Kauffman Roberts is senior rabbi of North Shore Temple Emanuel, a Progressive synagogue in Sydney, Australia. She has served as chair of the Assembly of Rabbis and Cantors of Australasia, been an active alumna of the Tisch Rabbinical Fellowship, and contributed writings to Rabbi Larry Hoffman's Prayers of Awe series, the *CCAR Journal*, Jewish Women International, the *Australian Jewish News*, and other publications. She was ordained by Hebrew Union College–Jewish Institute of Religion in Cincinnati in 2012.

Jonathan D. Sarna is the Joseph H. & Belle R. Braun Professor of American Jewish History at Brandeis University as well as chief historian of the Weitzman National Museum of American Jewish History. His many books include *American Judaism: A History* and *Coming to Terms with America*.

Yolanda Savage-Narva is the Assistant Vice President of Racial Equity, Diversity and Inclusion for the Union for Reform Judaism and the Religious Action Center. She has twenty years' experience working with public agencies and nonprofit organizations to promote equity and inclusion. Yolanda was also the Executive Director of Operation Understanding DC, a nonprofit organization dedicated to promoting understanding, cooperation, and respect while fighting to eradicate racism, anti-Semitism, and all forms of discrimination. She is a past Vice-Chair of the Commission on Social Action, a Senior Schusterman Fellow, a member of the Board of Directors for the Federation of Greater Washington, Capital Jewish Museum, Leading Edge, American Jewish World Services, the Historic Sixth and I Synagogue in Washington, DC, and an advisory member for the Tree of Life Memorial. Yolanda is also a member of Delta Sigma Theta Sorority, an international Black sorority dedicated to community service and education. She is a graduate of Tougaloo College and Jackson State University.

Joseph A. Skloot is the Rabbi Aaron D. Panken Assistant Professor of Modern Jewish Intellectual History and associate director of the Tisch Fellowship Program at Hebrew Union College–Jewish Institute of Religion. He is a historian of Jewish culture and religious thought and the author of *First Impressions:* Sefer Ḥasidim *and Early Modern Hebrew Printing* (Brandeis University Press, 2023).

Yael Splansky is the senior rabbi of Holy Blossom Temple in Toronto. She is the past president of the Toronto Board of Rabbis. She serves on the Beit Din of the Reform Rabbis of Greater Toronto and on the President's Rabbinic Council of Hebrew Union College-Jewish Institute of

Religion. She was a Vice President of the Central Conference of American Rabbis, editor of *Siddur Pirchei Kodesh,* and she is a Senior Rabbinic Fellow of the Shalom Hartman Institute. Splansky was recognized by Canadian Parliament with the Queen's Platinum Jubilee Award for her commitment to refugee relief, support and advocacy for the unhoused, and building bridges among faith communities. She has the unique privilege of being a fourth-generation Reform Rabbi. Together with Adam Sol, she raises three mensches.

Rachel Steiner is the senior rabbi at Barnert Temple in Franklin Lakes, New Jersey. While studying at HUC-JIR in New York, she took every class Rabbi Larry Hoffman offered and had the tremendous opportunity to work with him on her rabbinic thesis. She was ordained in 2010. Rachel grew up in New York City and graduated from the University of Pennsylvania in 2002. She and her husband are the grateful and lucky parents of Ezra and Asher.

David E. Stern is senior rabbi of Temple Emanu-El, Dallas, Texas. He was ordained by Hebrew Union College–Jewish Institute of Religion in 1989, where he also received an MA in Jewish education. He received his BA in English from Dartmouth College in 1983. He is a past president of the Central Conference of American Rabbis and currently serves on the Board of Governors of HUC-JIR. Stern's commentaries have appeared in the *Huffington Post* and *Haaretz.* His poetry and prose have appeared in the *CCAR Journal,* and he has contributed essays to four volumes on Jewish High Holiday liturgy edited by Rabbi Larry Hoffman: *Who by Fire, Who by Water: Un'taneh Tokef*; *All These Vows: Kol Nidre*; *May God Remember: Yizkor*; and *Naming God: Avinu Malkeinu.* Stern is married to Rabbi Nancy Kasten, and they have three children.

Gordon Tucker is vice chancellor for Religious Life and Engagement at the Jewish Theological Seminary and a senior fellow at the Shalom Hartman Institute of North America. He served as senior rabbi at Temple Israel Center in White Plains, New York, from 1994 to 2018 and is now senior rabbi emeritus. He holds an AB degree from Harvard College, a PhD from Princeton University, and rabbinic ordination from JTS. From 1984 to 1992, he was the dean of the JTS Rabbinical School, and from 1982 to 2007, he was a member of the Rabbinical Assembly Committee on Jewish Law and Standards. He has also been deeply involved in the cause of religious pluralism in Israel, through the Masorti Foundation, of which he is a past chairman. In 1979–80, he was a White House fellow and served as special assistant and chief speechwriter to US Attorney General Benjamin R. Civiletti. Tucker is married to Amy Cohn and has three children and five grandchildren.

Richard S. Vosko has worked as a liturgical design consultant for Christian and Jewish congregations throughout North America since 1970. He has provided dozens of consultations for Reform, Conservative, and Reconstructionist congregations in the United States and Canada. He served as a fellow and sacred space consultant for Synagogue 2000 and as a member of the Synagogue 3000 advisory board. Known internationally, Vosko is a frequent author and speaker on topics dealing with sacred art and architecture. His main research is concerned with how the built environment affects the behavior of congregations gathered for worship. He is currently interested in biomimetics and how religious buildings can be more ecologically efficient. His award-winning work continues to be featured in many architectural and art related journals. www.richardsvosko.com

Janet R. Walton is a musician, author, teacher, ritual leader, and professor emerita of worship and the arts at Union Theological Seminary in New York City. Since 1992, she has worked as a liturgical consultant with Jewish congregations to support possibilities for their work as liturgical leaders to expand traditions with an awareness and a commitment to meet current needs. After thirty-one years, she continues to meet monthly at Central Synagogue in New York City. With Rabbi Larry Hoffman, she has co-edited a book, taught naval chaplains, and helped students at Hebrew Union College–Jewish Institute of Religion to think about new ways of planning and leading worship. She participated in the Hoffman family seder, revised every year, discussed articles, books, world events, and spoken with him about "what ifs," that is, what rituals could do, if only . . .

Deborah Waxman, the first woman rabbi to head a Jewish congregational union and a Jewish seminary, became president and CEO of Reconstructing Judaism in 2014. She has drawn on her training as a rabbi and historian to become the Reconstructionist movement's leading voice in the public square. Under Waxman's leadership, Reconstructing Judaism has undertaken major initiatives while building ever-stronger relationships with affiliated congregations and innovating Judaism. Waxman is creator and host of *Hashivenu*, a podcast about Judaism and resilience. She has taught at the Reconstructionist Rabbinical College since 2002, where she is the Aaron and Marjorie Ziegelman Presidential Professor. Her writing has appeared in the *Forward, Times of Israel, Philadelphia Inquirer*, Jewish Telegraphic Agency, and other news outlets, and she has published several academic papers. She is a graduate of Columbia University and of the Reconstructionist Rabbinical College. She earned a PhD in American Jewish history from Temple University.

Margaret Moers Wenig told her undergraduate professor Dr. Jacob Neusner that she wanted to become a rabbi, and he insisted she apply to Hebrew Union College–Jewish Institute of Religion to study with Drs. Eugene Borowitz and Larry Hoffman. That she did. Enriched by their profound teachings and mentorship, Wenig served a small New York City congregation for twenty-six years, where her commitments to tradition and innovation were both welcomed. She has been teaching at HUC-JIR in New York since 1985. Her focus on religious communication, through sermons and through the relationship between words and music in worship, reflects the enduring influences of her teachers Neusner, Borowitz, and Hoffman, as well as another undergraduate professor of liturgical theology, Dr. David Blumenthal, even when she disagrees with them. Wenig was elected to be the first Jewish president of the Academy of Homiletics.

Daniel G. Zemel serves as senior rabbi of Temple Micah in Washington, DC, a position he has held since 1983. He views his primary role at Micah to be cultural translator—grappling with the challenge of translating our inherited Judaism into a theology and practice that speaks to our place and time. Zemel pursued his undergraduate education at Brown University and his rabbinic education at Hebrew Union College-Jewish Institute of Religion in Jerusalem and New York. A native of Chicago, he received his earliest Jewish and secular education at the Anshe Emet Day School. He and his wife, Louise, are blessed with three children and three grandchildren. He regards the latter as his best friends. Zemel is a devoted, passionate, lifelong fan of the Chicago White Sox. His favorite pastimes include being in Israel, reading, and annually napping in his *succah* dreaming of a return trip to the World Series for his beloved team.